I0622833

The Posimistiq Mind

A Posimistiq Production

We put mental health at the center of every story.®

The Posimistiq Mind

Learn how to build a strong mind
to succeed in everyday life

*The 8 traits and easy-to-learn, proven techniques of
mentally strong and successful people*

Ali G. Moghadam

DEDICATION

This book is dedicated to my children so they can always hear me regardless of where I am.

I'd also like to thank my wife, family, and friends for all their input, help, review, and encouragement. Without them, this book would not have been possible.

Table of Contents

INTRODUCTION

Life is hard. Life is unfair. Life is there for the taking.
If you are dealing with personal challenges, family challenges, or health challenges, this book is for you.

If you are a family leader or business leader, and you are unsure how to lead the people that rely on you the most, this book is for you.

If you are stressed with your job, hate your job, don't have a job, or want to change careers, this book is for you.

If you are a student stressed with your workload, or a teacher struggling to lead and motivate your students, this book is for you.

If you are stressed with your finances, anxious, going through a breakup, afraid to fly on an airplane, afraid of needles, or having a mid-life crisis, this book is for you.

Ultimately, if you are a human being, this book is for you. We all have unique challenges that "seem" to make our lives difficult.

So why does it seem like you are one of the only ones, if not the only one, dealing with life's difficulties? Why does it seem like most people around you live happy and stress-free lives?

First, know that you are not alone. Most people are not stress-free, always happy, and living their best lives, even if that seems to be the case every time you turn on your television or scroll through social media.

But there are people who have figured out the "free and happy life" formula to live a happy and successful life, even as life continues to throw difficulties their way. So, it is possible.

Then how do the "lucky" few do it? It is not as if sustained success or happiness can be bought at a store or solved by taking drugs (prescription/recreational), even if it temporarily creates a state of happiness.

These people did it, and continue to do it, by dedicating time to build their *mental strength*.

What is mental strength?

When I was younger, I always associated the word "strength" with the physical aspects of the body and what others could see. For me, strength was building strong arms, chest, back, legs, and abs. I never once thought of building strength in my mind. But I've come to realize that the most important strength to build is, in fact, the strength in a person's mind.

Mental strength is not a God-given talent. It is not black or white in that you have it or you don't.

Yes, we all have different starting points and baselines that we are working from. But just like our physical strengths, anyone can get mentally stronger than they were the previous day, month, or year, relative to themselves. They just have to learn how to do it and practice it consistently.

Picture the weightlifter at the gym, the marathon runner, or the professional athlete. All of these people have gradually developed their skills over time through learning, practice, and dedication.

Therefore, just as people spend time training their bodies to build physical strength, you must have the same dedication to train your mind to build mental strength.

Just think about it. Would you run a marathon without training? Would you be able to compete in the Olympics without training? Would you be able to perform heart surgery without training? Would you be able to do anything well without first learning "how to," then practicing what you learned, and remaining dedicated to your practice over time?

Developing mental strength, developing the Posimistiq Mind, can be achieved by anyone who wants to accomplish this. This book will teach you how so you can successfully navigate all that life throws your way.

Book structure

Throughout my life, I have had the privilege of crossing paths with various successful individuals who have excelled in their respective fields. These individuals come from diverse backgrounds, have faced unique challenges, and have had varying circumstances. From CEOs, business owners, doctors, and lawyers, to athletes, coaches, teachers, and immigrants, to my own family and friends, I have closely studied their journeys and the journeys of successful public figures in an attempt to decipher what led each person to achieve their level of success and happiness. What I have observed is that despite the differences in their experiences, each of these individuals demonstrates a set of core mental characteristics that contribute to success and happiness.

This book is a culmination of everything I've learned and it condenses a lifetime of accumulated knowledge into a digestible format designed to expedite your learning curve. It provides insights and strategies derived from the experiences of successful individuals, as well as my journey, backed by research and analyses, that can help you build the mental strength required for a lifetime of success and happiness.

Each chapter of the Posimistiq Mind is structured around one of eight *traits* of mental strength critical to your success. The focus is not just on identifying these traits but also on providing proven *techniques* that you can use to develop each trait. To put everything in perspective, each chapter provides numerous examples of highly successful people who have utilized these very same techniques and ways of thinking.

The goal of this book is to go beyond just providing you with the traits and techniques to achieve success. The goal is to offer suggestions and recommendations for implementing these techniques into your daily life. After reading each chapter, you won't be left wondering how to put what you've learned into practice.

Remember, it is still up to you to engrain these traits into your mind and work on the techniques daily. By taking these steps, you'll begin to grow mentally stronger so you can overcome your present-day challenges, prepare yourself to successfully handle all that life might throw at you in the future, and reach your full potential.

With that aspiration in mind, we end each chapter with a few brief propositions in the form of quotes. You can use these quotes as they are or adapt them for challenges specific to you, whether they involve health, safety, education, money, employment, entertainment, or something else.

Keys to success

Before you begin the first chapter, I encourage you to take a moment and think about the three things that are bothering you the most in life. As you read through each chapter, learn about each trait and learn about each technique; then think about how you can apply what you learned to what you are currently going through.

After you finish the book, leave the book in a place where you'll always see it. It could be your bookshelf, nightstand, work bag, school bag, office, or anywhere you will see the cover and title frequently. This is one simple technique to keep the Posimistiq Mind traits and techniques at the front of your mind daily. Reread the book from time to time. Just like you never forget how to ride a bike, it still takes continuous practice to operate the bike at peak performance. The same goes for building a strong mind.

Building a strong mind is not easy. It takes work, and it's hard. But it is possible if you commit to betting on yourself and being willing to fail before you succeed.

People who possess, work on daily, and utilize the traits and techniques of the Posimistiq Mind can achieve any level of success, any level of happiness, and anything they desire.

Portmanteau

Are you familiar with what a portmanteau is (pronounced: /pôrt ˈmantō/)? It is a word that blends the sounds and combines the meanings of multiple words.

For example, when I was in college, I could never get up early enough to eat breakfast at a normal hour. If I waited until lunchtime to eat my first meal of the day, I would become extremely hangry (the portmanteau of "hungry" and "angry"). Hence, to this day, my favorite meal is brunch (the portmanteau of "breakfast" and "lunch").

Can you guess what the origin of Posimistiq is? The origin of Posimistiq is simply the blend of the words and meanings of positive, optimistic, and "IQ."

You may be thinking, what is the difference between positive and optimistic? Positive is about "self-talk" and how you address the *present* moment. Optimistic is about looking at a situation you may be facing and remaining hopeful about what can happen in the *future*.

For example, it's very common for people to be unsatisfied and unfulfilled with their jobs. A negative and weak-minded thought process is thinking, "I hate my job," "I hate my career," "I'm not paid enough money," "I am so bored," and "This is what I am going to have to do for the rest of my life."

However, a positive thought process would be thinking, "I am grateful that I can work and make an income currently. I recognize it's a privilege to work and have an opportunity to make a living that many other people do not have." (Notice the positive thinking associated with the present moment.) If the person is also optimistic, they might think, "Even though I am grateful for this opportunity, I am still going to learn new skills and keep trying to find a career that is more in line with what fulfills me because I'm hopeful there are better things that lie ahead for me."

Posimistiq ends with the letters "IQ." The term IQ is short for intelligence quotient. When most people hear the word IQ, they associate it with a powerful brain and a strong mind. This is exactly what you are building with the Posimistiq Mind. You are building the strongest mind to successfully navigate all the challenges that life can throw your way.

The blend of these three words and meanings together into Posimistiq creates one of the most powerful portmanteaus and one of the most powerful mantras to help you build and sustain mental strength, not only for the present but also for the future.

Get to know your brain

Before you build anything, you must know what you are building and how to put the pieces together. Therefore, before you begin to build a stronger mind, you must be familiar with how your brain is built.

At a high level, your brain can be divided into three main parts: the cerebrum, cerebellum, and the brainstem.

If you dig a little deeper, the largest part of the brain, and the one most people visualize when they are asked to visualize a brain, is the cerebrum.

The cerebrum can be broken down into two hemispheres: the left and the right. Each of the hemispheres can be further broken down into four lobes: the frontal, parietal, occipital, and temporal lobes.

Have I lost you already? Well, this is all you need to know: Within each lobe, within each hemisphere, within the cerebrum, within the cerebellum, and within the brainstem, your brain controls everything from your personality, behavior, emotions, and sense of touch, to processing signals from vision, understanding language, memory, sequencing, and organizing.

In other words, there are very complex relationships between the lobes of the brain, between the right and left hemispheres, and between the cerebrum, cerebellum, and brainstem, which, together, control who you are.

Here is the point: While each part of the brain serves its unique purpose, the brain cannot function highly unless each part is working seamlessly together with the rest.

The same goes for developing a stronger mind. As you read through this book, you need to visualize yourself putting the eight pieces of the Posimistiq Mind together, chapter by chapter, trait by trait, and technique by technique.

The great philosopher Aristotle once said:

> *"The whole is greater than the sum of its parts."*

If you take all the parts of a watch and put them on a table, you will not be able to tell time. If you separate a car's engine from its wheels, you will not be able to travel. If you ate all the ingredients of your favorite meal individually, surely it would no longer be your favorite meal.

The same thought process can be applied to building a strong mind. You can build mental strength by working on and developing one or two traits. But developing only one or a few traits will not have the same impact on your life as developing all eight traits. The only way to build the strongest mind and maximize your success is to work on, piece together, and develop all eight traits of the Posimistiq Mind so they can work in tandem.

TRAIT 1

SHARE YOUR STORY

B e honest with yourself. What is your biggest mental struggle?

For most people, their biggest mental struggle has only gotten harder to deal with over time. It creates a mental fog, which only gets thicker and seems crippling most days. It slowly weakens your mind until one day, you wake up and don't even understand how you got there. You wonder what happened to that happy, stress-free, full-of-life person you once knew.

Maybe your struggle is associated with anxiety, depression, fear, stress, trauma, insecurity, or jealousy. Maybe it's related to addiction, grief or loss, family or relationship issues, career dissatisfaction, perfectionism, time management, loneliness, imposter syndrome, financial stress, parenting, or anger management. Or maybe it is the feeling of not being good enough, rich enough, thin enough, beautiful enough, happy enough, or _____ enough.

Whatever your current struggle is, you are not alone. Each person in your family has a struggle. Each of your friends is dealing with something. Every mentally strong person navigates mental challenges daily, even if you do not know about it.

Some of the most accomplished people are going through something like you, including NFL stars Steve Young, Lane Johnson, and Brandon Brooks; NBA star Kevin Love; Olympic gold medalists Michael Phelps and Simone Biles; Grammy award-winning and nominees Adele, Lady Gaga, and Demi Lovato; actors Ryan Reynolds, Dwayne Johnson, and Angelina Jolie; and comedian Kevin Hart. At some point in their lives, all of these people publicly shared and discussed a mental challenge they have dealt with and, for some, continue to deal with. The list goes on and on, and it continues to grow.

There is a reason why people continue to open up about their challenges and their quest to normalize mental health in this world. It is because people who have shared their stories knew it was the critical first step to successfully navigating their challenges and building a stronger mind.

There is a common phrase that has been reiterated by many motivational speakers, self-help authors, and countless other successful people. Its origin can be traced back to notable figures such as Aristotle and Roman Emperor Aurelius:

"Through adversity, you find your greatest strength."

Consider all the adversity, challenges, troubles, and obstacles you have already overcome in your life. Did they make you weaker or stronger? Most likely, they made you stronger.

The point is, if you want to develop mental strength, you must confront your greatest adversity or the story you are hiding. This is the story that you keep inside and feel hesitant to share with others, including those closest to you, because you think it will portray you as weak.

Sun Tzu, a Chinese military general, philosopher, and author of *The Art of War*, once said:

"Every battle is won before it's ever fought."

For your mental strength-building journey, this means that before you even begin to build mental strength, you must overcome your insecurities and be willing to share your story. Only then can you confidently step into the battle of building mental strength, ready to emerge victorious.

This is why sharing your story is the first trait in building the Posimistiq Mind. If you don't share your greatest adversity, then you will never be able to find your greatest strength.

Even though it is the first trait to master, it might not necessarily be easy. It might be the hardest trait to master, but it will also be the most influential in developing the mental strength to achieve the happiness and success you desire.

Once you share your story, you will realize that it is healing and therapeutic. It is critical in your journey. It will allow you to rid yourself of those demons and get back to living life the way you once knew.

When you share your story, you will feel like a huge weight has been lifted. When you have the feeling of less weight on your shoulders, this allows you to build a stronger mind.

To make it easier to share their stories, the strongest-minded people realize they are not alone in their struggles. They realize they are not the first to experience their challenges, and they will not be the last.

To *motivate* yourself to overcome your insecurities and share your story, use the following five techniques:

1. Cut through the vulnerability paradox.
2. Never watch a scary movie alone.
3. Know that sharing your weakness does not make you weak.
4. Remember that you could save someone you love.
5. Realize there's no wrong way to share your story.

Always remember, we all have a story to share regardless of who we are. Do not be afraid to share your story, regardless of what it is.

Cut through the vulnerability paradox

Sharing your story is hard because it requires you to be vulnerable. Vulnerability is defined by Oxford Languages as the quality or state of being exposed to the possibility of being attacked or harmed, either physically or emotionally.

No wonder we hesitate to be vulnerable! Why would anyone want to proactively do something that puts themselves at higher risk of being attacked, damaged, or wounded? When we are vulnerable, we risk getting laughed at or rejected. We feel our reputations, friendships, and relationships could be at risk. We're afraid that our vulnerability and our stories will make us look weak.

But have you ever thought about how your perception of vulnerability in yourself is drastically different from your perception of vulnerability in others? Brené Brown describes this paradox in her best-selling book, *Daring Greatly: How the Courage to be Vulnerable Changes the Way We Live, Love, and Parent*:

> *"During my talk, I asked the audience two questions that reveal so much about the many paradoxes that define vulnerability.*
>
> *"First, I asked, 'How many of you struggle to be vulnerable because you think of vulnerability as weakness?' Hands shot up across the room.*
>
> *"Then I asked, 'When you watched people on this stage being vulnerable, how many of you thought it was courageous?' Again, hands shot up across the room..."*

The paradox is we admire vulnerability in others, but we resist it within ourselves. We view vulnerability as a strength for others but a weakness within ourselves.

Mentally strong people cut through this paradox and fully embrace their vulnerabilities. They let themselves be seen by the world as they truly are. They know that being vulnerable and sharing their story allows them to make space for growth, that their relationships with other people will strengthen, and that they will begin to meet people who will be able to help them.

Consider this comment from Sundar Pichai, CEO of Alphabet and Google:

"Let yourself feel insecure from time to time. It will help you grow as an individual."

The first step on your journey to sharing your story and building mental strength is to let yourself be vulnerable. Let yourself be seen and give yourself the same credit you give others when they are vulnerable with you. Your level of transparency with others is key to your resilience and ability to build mental strength moving forward.

Never watch a scary movie alone

Do you remember the first scary movie you ever saw? Did it involve a monster, a killer lurking in the house, ghosts, or something else? Regardless of which movie it was and the differences in characters, settings, storylines, and time, scary movies are almost always structured the same way:

1. The protagonists are happy, excited, and unafraid.
2. They encounter a threat.
3. They struggle with that threat.
4. Some finally escape the threat.

In other words, in the beginning, the protagonists are typically happy, carefree, full of life, and unafraid, and it's usually sunny without a cloud in the sky.

As the movie progresses, sunny skies slowly turn to clouds, nightfall approaches, the weather begins to turn, the rain gets heavier by the minute, and the sounds of thunder get louder.

The characters begin to see, hear, and experience things that are "off". Finally, after the pressure has built up over an extended period, we find ourselves watching the pinnacle of the struggle.

Screenwriters structure scary movies this way because they know they need to give us time to let our minds wander, let us get in our heads, let our hearts race, and let the pressure build. They know fear and anxiety do not happen instantly but are instead built up over time.

If you think about it, this seems eerily like life. We are all living in different settings, have our unique plots, and are dealing with characters specific to our lives. But despite all the differences, our lives are structured the same way.

As young children, we are happy, carefree, stress-free, and unafraid. As we progress through life, we begin to see and hear things that slowly build our anxieties and fears. At one point or another, we *all* find ourselves at the climax of our struggles, the scariest part of our movies, trying to escape. This might be where you are at today.

Now think about the last scary movie you saw. Did you watch the movie alone, or did you watch it with someone else?

Most people don't think about watching a scary movie alone, let alone actually do it. You know that you need someone else there with you to support you, go through the experience with you, and bring you back to reality by reminding you it is just a movie. You need that support to make you feel better, to help you get to the end of the movie when the threat is no longer there, and to allow relief to finally settle in.

If you wouldn't watch a scary movie alone, then why would you ever try to get through your own life's scary movie alone?

The root cause of most challenges in life, most weaknesses, most anxieties, and most depressions, can all be traced back to fear.

Fear comes in all shapes and forms: the fear of failure, flying, needles, spiders, losing a loved one, dying, public speaking, heights, social settings, infertility, financial instability, disappointing those we love, or not reaching our goals.

What is your biggest fear? What are you keeping to yourself? What is your biggest mental struggle? Finish this sentence:

"My biggest fear is _____."

Now think about that fear for a moment. Is your heart beating a little faster? Have you gotten a little more anxious? That is because fear is an anxious feeling caused by our anticipation and perception of an imagined event or experience. In other words, you are making your own scary movie!

Here is the point: In the end, reality is not as bad as we perceive it to be. When you are lost in your movie and lost in your head, you just need to find a way back to what is real.

Every person has a scary movie unique to themselves. But mentally strong people don't try to experience their scary movies alone. They turn to others for support.

So, if you picked up this book because you think, *"I'm living in the wrong movie,"* or *"I need to get out of this scary movie,"* begin to share your story with others so they can support you in life, just like they supported you during the scary movie.

Sharing your weakness does not make you weak

We are conditioned throughout our lives to associate weakness with being inadequate and that no good can come from weakness. Usually, the weak team loses, the weak employee gets fired, the weak business fails, and the weak animal doesn't survive.

This is why most people pride themselves on only sharing what they are good at. Most people downplay their failures and are afraid to share their stories. We've been conditioned to think our stories make us look weak. But as you've already learned, it's a common misconception that showing vulnerability is a sign of weakness. In reality, it's an essential part of being human.

Consider the example of Dwayne "The Rock" Johnson, one of the physically strongest and most successful individuals in the world. Despite his seemingly invincible persona, he has spoken openly about the importance of seeking help and support during difficult times. In his own words,

> *"I've found that one of the most important things you could realize is that you are not alone... I wish I had someone at that time who could just pull me aside and say, 'Hey, it is gonna be okay. It will be okay.'"*

The irony is that even someone who appears to be almost indestructible can still feel the weight of emotional struggles and can benefit from sharing his story with others.

Recognize that sharing your story does not make you weak; it makes you human. It is human nature to avoid showing your weaknesses. Publicly admitting your failures, mistakes, and challenges is not what we as humans prefer to do. It doesn't feel natural. This makes sharing your weaknesses harder than it should be.

But failing to recognize your weaknesses prevents you from living up to your full potential. When you share your weaknesses with others, you take the pressure off trying to be perfect. You build courage because you just did something that is naturally hard. Building courage only strengthens your mind, which will help you navigate through future challenges.

Additionally, it is when you share your weaknesses that you embrace the support of others. In times of strength, we trick our minds into thinking we do not need the help of others. We trick ourselves into thinking we can do everything in life alone. But going through life alone will only get you so far.

Have you ever heard the phrase, *"If you want to go fast, go alone, but if you want to go far, go together"*? To go "together," you need to have incredible bonds with other people. Unfortunately, incredible bonds are not formed in times of strength. Incredible bonds are formed in times of shared weaknesses and struggles. Consider the following examples:

- During a natural disaster like a hurricane, people in the affected area often come together to help each other despite differences in background, race, or socioeconomic status.

- In a family, a crisis such as a health scare or financial hardship can bring members closer together as they rally around each other for support.
- In a sport, a team that is struggling to win games may initially experience tension and conflict among its members. But as they work together to improve their performance and support each other through losses, they can form a strong bond that helps them achieve success in the future.
- In a workplace setting, a team that is struggling to meet a tight deadline may initially experience tension and conflict as the members work under pressure. But as they collaborate and rely on each other to complete the project, they may form a cohesive and supportive bond that allows them to work well together in the future.

These examples demonstrate how shared experiences of weakness or vulnerability can lead to the formation of strong bonds between individuals, groups, teams, and communities.

To build mental strength, you must associate sharing your weaknesses with an opportunity to build relationships and incredible amounts of trust with other people.

When you share your weaknesses with others, you become authentic. You show others the incredible levels of trust you have in them. The impact is powerful.

In turn, they will want to reciprocate by helping you overcome your weakness, helping you get further in life than you could have without them, and rooting for you along the way. You will also notice these very same people begin to open up to you about their weaknesses and struggles. When they do, you will build even stronger and deeper connections with them as you both embark on your journeys in building mental strength together.

Your greatest potential for strength can be found within your weaknesses. So, lead with your weaknesses, not your strengths. The irony is your weaknesses will lead you to your greatest strengths.

You could save someone you love

No matter how hard it is to share your story, remember your story may help someone close to you overcome an obstacle in his or her life. Without sharing your story, that person may continue to struggle.

Think about it. When given a choice, would you rather have someone close to you, such as a child, parent, sibling, or friend, feel pain? Or would you rather have the power to take that pain away?

Most people prefer to take that pain away from a loved one, even if that means they must take that pain on themselves.

You may not know it, but you have the power to help someone close to you. All you must do is share your story, no matter how painful it seems.

By openly sharing your imperfections, you inform others who struggle that they are not alone. You inspire them to think, "If they can, then maybe I can too" and give them the courage to keep moving forward.

You never know when one of your stories will serve as the catalyst for others to recognize what they're going through, to get help, and to live better lives.

Mentally strong and successful people are brave enough to step out of their comfort zones and share their stories because they know these could help lead their loved ones out of their darkness.

Hopefully, just knowing that your story can save a loved one will inspire you to become vulnerable and share your story.

There's no wrong way to share your story

When you feel like you are ready to share your story, you might be thinking, "I don't know how to share it."

There is no perfect moment or perfect way to share your story. Consider the words of French philosopher and writer Voltaire:

"Do not let perfection be the enemy of good."

It means that sometimes, in the pursuit of perfection, you may end up sacrificing progress or even settle for nothing at all, instead of striving for something good that is achievable. This quote serves as a reminder that it is better to strive for progress and improvement, rather than holding out for an unattainable perfection. Do not let perfection prevent you from implementing everything you just prepared yourself for. It does not need to be perfect. It just needs to be done.

It is your journey, so tell it however it feels right to you at that moment. It could be face-to-face with just one person. It could be face-to-face with a group of people. It could be over the phone, through video chat, or text message. It could be shared through social media or by writing a letter. It could be shared with a close relative or with a professional in mental health.

Life will open up to you when you are able to embrace the ride and be a part of it. And when you least expect it, something great might come along, better than you even planned for.

Mentally strong and successful people do not dwell on finding the perfect way to share their stories. Instead, they get their stories out as soon as possible, so they can start building the mental strength to conquer all that life has to offer, while also helping others. In other words, just do it!

Finally, as we wrap up this chapter, if you are currently struggling, feeling mentally weak, or feeling like there is no hope or chance for a brighter future, consider this comment from Tyler Perry. He overcame numerous challenges in his life, including poverty and abuse, to become a successful actor, writer, producer, and director:

"I know it may seem like there is no hope. But please reach out to someone. Share your story.

"What I realized now is looking back on all those dark times, sometimes you just need to buy into the pain. That's the way I had to look at it to get through it.

"I wouldn't have been able to find the happiness that I found today had I given up through all that pain, all that struggle. If I had given up, I wouldn't have seen the better part of my life.

"Please, think about what that other side could be. It could be amazing. And you missed the best part of it not going through the darkness. Don't let the darkness stop you from getting to the incredible place of light. I'm a living witness, you can make it through."

– Tyler Perry

TRAIT 2

FIND YOUR PURPOSE

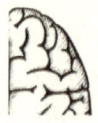

It's Sunday night. The sun begins to set. Your glorious, happy, and fun weekend is coming to an end. You spent the last 48 hours doing things you wanted to do. But tomorrow is Monday, and the reality is you must go back to work. The Sunday Scaries begin to set in.

You brush your teeth, get into your pajamas, shut off the lights, and get into bed. Unable to fall asleep, you keep thinking to yourself, "I cannot go back to the grind of another work week. I cannot go back to that desk for another week. How am I going to go work for that boss I hate, the team I do not get along with, the angry customer yelling at me, the patient coughing in my face, or the mission I do not connect with?" The minutes tick by until you finally drift off to sleep later than you would have liked. And just like that, Monday morning is here.

As you go through the motions of the week, why does it seem like other people are not stuck on autopilot? How do these people have energy? Why do they always look fresh, no matter the day of the week?

These mentally strong people have identified their purpose and their reason to get up in the morning, and they stay connected to their purpose with what they do daily. Even if they're doing something they don't enjoy, they stay connected to their purpose to remind themselves of why they are doing it in the first place.

The best businesses, the best professionals, the best parents, and the best of anything are all connected to a purpose.

Once you can clearly define your purpose, no matter what you are faced with, no matter what day of the week it is, you will have the *fuel* necessary to power you through any of life's challenges.

But finding your purpose is hard. Finding your purpose takes time. Most people struggle to find their purpose. Most people do not even know where to look to find it. Even mentally strong people who have found their purpose experienced these very same challenges during their journey to define their purpose.

So how did they find it, and how can you find yours?

Three-way intersection

Sara Blakely, the founder of Spanx, said:

> *"It's very important to know your purpose because if you start with "why" and stay connected to the "why," it's going to fuel you. If you have a purpose and it's bigger than yourself, then you'll survive the ups and downs. Your purpose is your anchor.*

FIND YOUR PURPOSE

"Purpose is simply three things. It's at the intersection of these three questions:

1. *What do you enjoy?*
2. *What are you good at?*
3. *How do you want to serve the world (i.e., What breaks your heart?)?"*

It's this technique to define her purpose that inspired Blakely to create the company Spanx, ultimately leading to her becoming the youngest self-made female billionaire at the time.

To put this in perspective, when you do something you enjoy, it creates an energizing feedback loop that will fuel your productivity.

When you do something you are good at, it creates an easier experience. We all gravitate toward things we are good at because of the satisfaction we feel from success. In turn, this adds to the energizing feedback loop that continues to fuel productivity.

What breaks your heart, or what you truly care about, will drive you to turn pain into purpose. Pain has a powerful way of teaching us what is most important in our lives.

For example, if you have ever lost a loved one, you know how your perspective on life changed from that moment on. You might have gotten involved in more fundraisers, such as 5k runs, bake sales, car washes, or blood drives, or otherwise helped to raise money to support a cause such as beating cancer, suicide prevention, or mental health awareness.

These events take hours to prepare and coordinate. The people coordinating the events and the people participating in the events usually don't do it for money. They participate because something in their past broke their hearts, and they are motivated to prevent it from happening to someone else in the future. They are motivated to change the world, even if it's in a small way.

Here's a key point. Don't fall into the trap of associating money with your purpose. While money can make your life easier, it will not necessarily make you happier. How many times have you heard the stories about the finance professional or the rich person with hundreds of thousands, millions, or even billions of dollars in the bank, who was still unfulfilled and unhappy?

There are numerous studies that show money alone will not make you happy. In fact, many billionaires have joined the Giving Pledge, which is a promise by the world's wealthiest individuals and families to dedicate the *majority* of their wealth to charitable causes.

Created by Warren Buffet, Melinda Gates, and Bill Gates, the Giving Pledge has signatures (i.e., commitments) from over 235 people residing in 28 different countries as of the time of this publication. These individuals include Mackenzie Scott, Mark Zuckerberg, Brian Armstrong, Sheikh Dr. Mohammed Bin Musallam Bin Ham Al-Ameri, Shamsheer and Shabeena Vayalil, Sara Blakely, and others.

These people realized they do not need all that money to live a purposeful and fulfilled life.

This doesn't mean money doesn't matter. Of course, it's critical to know how to make an income, but it should not be your only focus when defining your purpose. For example, Sara Blakely didn't start her career to become a billionaire. Rather, she discovered her talent and passion for sales and had the desire to enhance women's hosiery, which was her way of serving the world. Her purpose was to create something of value that would benefit others. The wealth she accumulated was simply a natural outcome of pursuing her purpose. Ultimately, if you follow your purpose, the money will follow.

With that in mind, consider the following three questions and write down three answers for each.

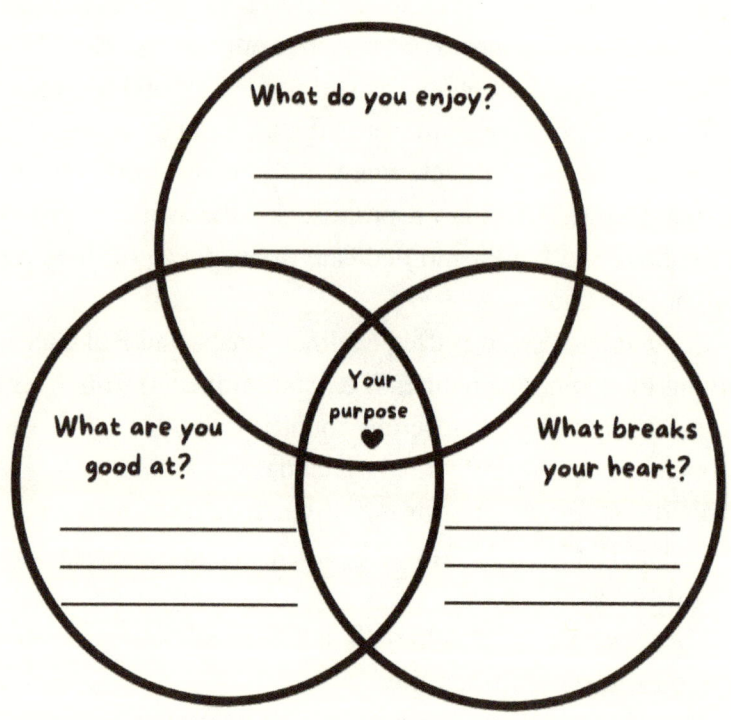

Can you think of any type of job or purpose where all three answers overlap? Are there connections between supporting your family and loved ones, supporting your community, fighting for social causes, helping children, helping those less fortunate, making the world a better place for the next generation, building businesses that positively impact people's lives, or something else? Even something as simple as being a great parent or living authentically is purposeful. For example:

- I *enjoy* helping people achieve their full potential and more than they thought they were capable of.
- I am a *good* communicator who can make complex topics easy to understand.
- It *breaks my heart* to see someone struggling with a challenge to the point where it is mentally crippling, and I always feel the need to help.

It is at the intersection of these three bullets that led me to define my purpose of helping people build mental strength to live better lives.

If you cannot find any connection points right now, that's okay. You have only just been introduced to this technique. Remember, finding your purpose is hard and it takes time. Continue to keep these three questions at the front of your mind and keep refining your answers as needed. If you stay committed, at some point you'll find the intersection where all three points connect.

When in doubt, remember this quote by Donald Rumsfeld, the former U.S. Secretary of Defense, who stated:

> *"...there are 'known knowns' (i.e., things we know we know). We also know there are 'known unknowns'; that is to say we know there are some things we do not know. But there are also* **'unknown unknowns**,*' the ones we don't know we don't know..."*

The key takeaway is *you don't know what you don't know*. Therefore, if you cannot find the intersection of the three purpose questions, then your answer may lie within the unknown unknowns.

Do something that scares you every day

To help uncover your unknown unknowns, the most powerful technique is to do something that scares you every day. When we do things that scare us, we experience the most growth.

To put this in perspective, visualize the mental growth trajectory of a child compared to an adult. A child's brain is like a sponge because it absorbs everything that comes its way. Conversely, they say you cannot teach an old dog new tricks because the older you get, the more reluctant you are to learn new things and break old habits.

The biggest difference between a child's brain and an adult's brain is the response to fear and the unknown.

Think about it. Everything a child experiences is initially an "unknown unknown". Everything is initially out of his or her comfort zone. And while many children might cling to their parents or caregivers, cry, or resist trying something new at first,

30

those same children will eventually try new things because their parents or guardians encourage them to do so and face their fears.

Trying new things allows children to learn what they like, what they hate, and what they love.

Take a moment and think about some of your earliest childhood memories when you were scared to do something. Think about how those experiences taught you new things and opened your eyes to what you like, hate, and love to do. How different would you be today if you chose to run away from those scary feelings as a child?

Unfortunately, as we get older, we become more independent and rely less on others pushing us to face our fears. Our response to fear resides within our minds, and we have the authority to react to our own human instinct.

Human instinct is to keep yourself safe, avoid failure, and avoid fear. But that instinct goes too far when it causes you to only live in your comfort zone.

Living in your comfort zone prevents you from learning and discovering new things. If you stay in your comfort zone, your life will stay small and predictable. If you never try anything new, your mind won't be as strong as it could be. Living in your comfort zone is often where people begin to struggle mentally.

Mentally strong people associate fear and discomfort with bravery and strength. They recognize they cannot find their purpose by living in their comfort zones. Instead, they lean into the discomfort, and they find their purpose by trying things that scare them. They recognize that courage is about being afraid and doing it anyway.

Military personnel, who are considered to be some of the strongest-minded people, are excellent examples of people who encounter fears daily. Even though they may feel afraid in the heat of the moment, they recognize that their bravery and strength come not from being fearless, but from facing their fears head-on and doing what needs to be done despite their fears. By continuously confronting their fears, they serve their purpose of protecting their country and fellow soldiers.

Think about a time you were scared to do something as an adult, and you still ended up doing it. How much did you learn about yourself from that experience? How good did you feel after it was over? Did you want to do it again? Did it at least give you confidence and pride that you got through it?

Now, think about a time you were scared to do something and decided *not* to do it because of that fear. Did you pass on a job opportunity? Did you skip a vacation with family or friends to avoid flying? Did you stay in a bad relationship because it was comfortable? What did you gain from *not* doing something because it was scary?

As you try to find your purpose moving forward, try running toward the fear and staying uncomfortable. When you run away from the fear, your mind begins to weaken and you'll be less capable of handling life's challenges in the future. If you run toward the fear, the opposite will happen.

You will never know what your limits are until you try to push past your fears. Once you do that, you can start to navigate around and play within your limits. It is this mindset that will help you uncover your unknown unknowns.

While we can't uncover all of our blind spots, we can reduce them by doing something that scares us every day. Remember, there is always a little growth in discomfort. One day, your combination of experiences will lead you to your purpose.

Put on your "gap" glasses

If you're still struggling to see the answers to your purpose questions, considering your own mortality can be a powerful way to gain perspective, clarity, and inspiration toward your purpose.

Considering your own mortality is like putting on glasses that allow you to see your purpose with 20/20 vision. On one lens, you have your legacy, and on the other, you have your eulogy. The glasses will help you see the *gap* between where you are and where you want to be.

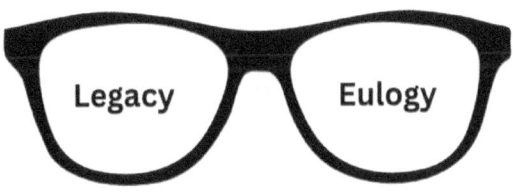

The "legacy" lens: Many people live in the present moment without thinking about how their legacy will live on after they pass away.

However, mentally strong people and successful people consider their legacies as a source of inspiration to find their present-day purpose. They visualize how their actions are going to affect their loved ones, their community, and the world, both now and in the future. This allows them to gain an incredible sense of perspective, clarity, and inspiration toward their life's purpose. Consider these comments from the following successful people:

- Arianna Huffington, a co-founder of the Huffington Post, said, *"When you start thinking about the legacy you want to leave behind, it helps you focus on what really matters in life and what your true purpose is."*
- Bill Gates, the founder of Microsoft, said, *"Thinking about my legacy helped me realize that my purpose in life is to use my talents and resources to make a positive difference in the world."*
- Gary Vaynerchuk, serial entrepreneur, and bestselling author, said, *"Your legacy is not just what you leave behind; it's what you live each day."*

Although it is an inevitability for all of us, many people tend to avoid contemplating their own mortality due to the fear it evokes. The subject can be daunting and unsettling, and it's understandable why a person may choose to suppress such thoughts.

But reflecting on your mortality is a critical technique in identifying any *gap* between the legacy you are currently leaving behind and the one you aspire to leave. This *gap* can provide the inspiration needed to define your purpose and pursue a more fulfilling life.

Just think about someone who has been given a limited amount of time to live due to illness. His or her perspective on life and what he or she wants to do completely shifts at that moment.

Take a moment right now and put yourself in that position. If you were told you only had one year left to live, what would you do differently today to solidify the legacy you want to leave behind? What mark do you want to leave on this world, even if it's just with one person or in a small way? How do you want to be remembered? For example, do you aspire to be a family-oriented individual who is always there for your loved ones? Or a successful businessperson who makes a positive impact on your industry and community? Perhaps you hope to be an advocate for a specific cause or a mentor/teacher who impacts the lives of everyone you work with.

Here is how you get closer to identifying your purpose. What would the answer to these questions be *if your life ended today?* It's in the gap between these sets of questions that will help you undertake a new approach to life to identify your purpose.

The "eulogy" lens: To be clear, legacy is not just about leaving behind material possessions or accomplishments but also about positively impacting and inspiring the people around you. Consider these comments from the following successful people:

- Sheryl Sandberg, a successful businesswoman and advocate for women's empowerment and gender equality in the workplace, said, *"When you focus on your legacy, it forces you to think beyond your own personal gain and think about the impact you can have on others."*
- Former President Barack Obama said, *"When you think about the legacy you want to leave behind, it gives your life purpose and meaning beyond your own individual success."*

So take the technique a step further by visualizing yourself in attendance at your own funeral. Think about the three people who will eulogize you to everyone else in attendance at your funeral. They could be immediate family members, extended family members, friends, coworkers, or those you have connected with in your community. What would each person say about you? Take a moment to imagine it now:

- Speaker one might say, "[*Insert your name*] was..."
- Speaker two might say, "I'm going to tell you all a story many of you have not heard before, but it's a true reflection of the type of person [*Insert your name*] was."
- And Speaker three might say, "Everyone probably knows [*Insert your name*] as _____, but to me he/she was..."

How do you feel about what each person just said? Do you take pride in what you instilled in each of their lives, or do you have any regret, wishing you could have influenced them differently? The *gap* between these questions can help lead you to your purpose.

Ultimately, when you confront your own mortality and recognize the brevity of life, as well as contemplate your legacy and the impact you are making on those closest to you, you can gain a clear 20/20 vision of the *gap* between where you are and where you want to be. This clarity can help you answer the three critical questions that will guide you toward your purpose.

The secret to staying motivated

Thinking about your purpose will only get you so far. When you keep your purpose to yourself, you lack accountability. Without accountability, it becomes easy to pivot, change course, procrastinate, or stop when life gets difficult.

You are far more likely to stay committed and achieve your purpose when you put your thoughts and goals out to the world. Putting your thoughts out to the world creates something you can be measured against. Measurement is a technique that creates accountability.

Peter Drucker, often referred to as the "father of modern management" and author of over 35 books on business management, famously stated:

"What gets measured, gets done."

For example, think about how much more motivated you are to study for an exam when you know you'll be graded (i.e., measured) on your performance from A to F. On the other hand, in a pass/fail class, you may not be as motivated to put in the effort required to learn and retain important information.

Mentally strong and successful people create measurement, accountability, and motivation by:

1. writing down their purpose, and
2. communicating their purpose to other people.

When you write down your purpose, you make it tangible. You can see your purpose right in front of you and keep yourself focused.

When you identify your purpose, write it down on a piece of paper. Keep it in your pocket or create a reminder on your cell phone. Make sure it's somewhere where you'll see it daily. These notes serve as your benchmark for measurement. Consider these words from Jack Canfield, author of the best-selling book series *Chicken Soup for the Soul*, who rephrases Peter Drucker's statement as:

"What gets written down, gets done."

When you fail to write things down, it becomes much easier for you to change course. It's much easier and faster to change a thought than to change something that is written down. Thoughts take milliseconds to form, but erasing and rewriting things take longer.

While writing down your purpose is extremely effective, communicating your purpose to others is even more motivating. When you tell your family, friends, and others your goals or how you want to live a certain way, these people can measure you against your commitment. You create accountability, which makes it harder for you to quit.

Communicating your purpose also enables those you care about to provide you encouragement along your journey. If they do not know your purpose, then they have no way of helping you.

When you tell someone else what you plan to do, you are creating the motivation for yourself that will propel you forward. Everyone has an internal desire to deliver on their commitments.

Think about the last time you told someone you were going to do something. Did you end up doing it, or did you quit? How would your answer change if you had kept your goals to yourself?

Even if you fail, you'll end up further along in your journey than you would have if you kept your goals to yourself.

Once you define your purpose, tell someone. You can start small with one person you trust. But over time, be sure to share your purpose with more people you look up to and respect. You are much more likely to persist when you share it with someone you respect, as opposed to someone you do not care much about.

Always live up to your own expectations

After doing all the work we discussed in this chapter, you now have a little more clarity into who you are, and you've begun to identify your "why," your values, and your purpose. The only thing left to do now is live up to your own expectations!

Remember to remain focused on the things that are aligned with your purpose and filter out anything that is not. When you are faced with a difficulty in life or have a tough decision to make, consider your purpose and your own expectations for yourself. And if someone undermines or causes you to doubt your purpose, consider this story that serves as a powerful reminder to live up to your expectations and to seek out places and people that value you for who you are.

A father said to his daughter, "You have graduated with honors. Here is a car I bought many years ago. It is pretty old now. But before I give it to you, take it to the used car lot downtown and tell them I want to sell it and see how much they offer you for it."

The daughter went to the used car lot, returned to her father, and said, "They offered me only $100 because they said it looks pretty worn out."

The father said, "Now take it to the pawn shop." The daughter went to the pawn shop, returned to her father, and said, "The pawn shop offered $1,000 because it is an old car."

The father then asked his daughter to go to a car club and show them the car. The

*daughter took the car to the club, returned,
and told her father, "Some people in the club
offered $100,000 for it because it's a Nissan
Skyline R34. It's an iconic car and sought by
many collectors!"*

*Now the father said this to his daughter,
"The right place values you the right way. If
you are not valued, do not be angry. It means
you are in the wrong place. Those who know
your value are those who appreciate you.
Never stay in a place where no one sees your
value."*

The author of this story is unknown, but it is a popular anecdote that has been shared by many motivational speakers and successful people.

TRAIT 3

SILENCE THE NOISE

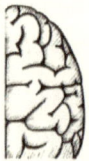

It was 3:24 p.m. on January 15, 2009. By all accounts, it was a typical winter day in New York City. The air was brisk - about 20 degrees Fahrenheit - and there were a few clouds in the sky. US Airways Flight 1549 was cleared for takeoff.

Less than three minutes later, Captain Sullenberger radioed a mayday call.

> *"...this is Cactus fifteen thirty-nine, hit birds. We've lost thrust on both engines. We're turning back...unable...we can't do it...we're gonna be in the Hudson."*

Are you familiar with this story? It's known as the Miracle on the Hudson. On that day, when faced with no engine power and a life-or-death situation, Captain Chesley Sullenberger (aka Captain Sully) and First Officer Jeffrey Skiles successfully landed the Airbus A320, originally bound for Charlotte, North Carolina, in the Hudson River, saving all 150 passengers and three flight attendants on board.

Sullenberger later said:

> *"It was very quiet as we worked, my copilot Jeff Skiles and I. We were a team. But to have zero thrust coming out of those engines was shocking – the silence."*

I encourage you to listen to the cockpit audio from the time of the bird strike until the landing. The QR code below will take you directly to the recording.

As you listen to the recording, pay attention to Captain Sully's poise and level of calm. Notice how he is not screaming, panicking, or making impulse decisions. It even seems like he is calmer than the air traffic controllers he is speaking with, even though he is the one flying the airplane. _More importantly, pay attention to the amount of silence._ Even as questions are being asked, he responds with only what is needed in the moment, a one-word answer, or no response at all.

At one point (around the 40-second mark) in the three-minute ordeal, there are 25 seconds of continuous silence, then just a simple one-word answer - "unable" - followed by another 15 seconds of silence from Captain Sully.

Note: In case the link is no longer active at the time you are reading this, you can also find multiple recordings of the audio by simply searching for "Captain Sullenberger US Airways flight 1549 audio transcript" on Google or YouTube.

Did you notice the air traffic control providing Captain Sully with multiple options within those three minutes?

In the end, in the direst situation, Captain Sully exhibited one of the most important traits of a mentally strong person: silencing the noise. He did not impulsively take the first or second option that was presented to him. He silenced all that noise, so he could use the time to focus on what was best for him and everyone else on the plane and make the best decision.

What is mental noise?

Throughout your day, you will encounter many distractions. These distractions may relate to how you should be thinking, feeling, and living, and what you should be doing and buying.

Distractions come from external sources, such as your friends and family, your job, meetings, school, enemies, media, advertisements, technology, social media, email, and your phone.

Distractions also come from within, such as your inner monologue providing you a constant flow of often irrelevant thoughts, dwelling on the past, worrying about the future, daydreaming, the comparison trap, pursuit of perfection, desire for wealth, or having FOMO (fear of missing out).

All these constant streams of thoughts, worries, and distractions create noise in your mind. The more distractions you encounter, the louder the noise becomes.

Noise makes it difficult to focus, and it impairs your ability to effectively process information. Noise pulls you in all directions, making you unproductive, stressed, and anxious. Noise distracts you from true happiness and success.

Mentally strong people turn down the volume and silence the noise to maximize happiness and success. They work hard in silence, and only let their success be their noise.

Relentless focus

Silencing the noise begins with focus. In fact, the key to success is focus. The most productive people have relentless focus by mastering their attention and filtering out distractions. They do less, but with more focus, which leads to better outcomes. Take, for example, a quote from Bill Gates:

> *"My success, part of it certainly, is that I have focused on a few things."*

Relentless focus requires uninterrupted time to zero in on your key priorities that make the most difference in your life.

So how can you develop relentless focus? First, to narrow your life's focus, begin with the "punch card" technique, which Warren Buffet, a famed investor, often shares in his lectures at business schools. He said:

> *"I could improve your ultimate financial welfare by giving you a ticket with only 20 slots in it so that you had 20 punches, representing all the investments that you got to make in a lifetime. And once you'd punched through the card, you couldn't make any more investments at all."*

Charlie Munger, Vice-Chairman of Berkshire Hathaway, who has worked closely with Buffet for many years, further expands on Buffet's quote by saying:

> *"To me, it's obvious that the winner has to bet very selectively. It's been obvious to me since very early in life. I don't know why it's not obvious to many other people."*

While this technique is about success in financial investments, the mindset that is derived from it can be applied to develop relentless focus and a strong mind. The technique compels you to be *highly selective*. It compels you to be focused on fewer things.

Once you have narrowed your focus, achieving relentlessness is all about mastering the art of time management.

Think of yourself as a horologist of time management, a master of time. Just as a horologist carefully pieces together the various materials in a watch to produce a harmonious, silent timepiece, people who are skilled at time management can organize, allocate, and prioritize their time to maximize their success.

Visualize the items on your punch card as your watch case, which is the shield surrounding the other three silencing elements of time management, which are:

1. Investing
2. Buying
3. Deciding

If you can piece these elements together, you will develop relentless focus and a strong and unbeatable mind. As Lee Iacocca, a revolutionary automotive industry executive, said:

> *"The ability to concentrate and to use your time well is everything if you want to succeed in business, or almost anywhere else for that matter."*

Relentless Focus

Invest in time blocking

Mentally strong and successful people view time as a currency. Have you ever heard of the phrase, "Time is your most valuable asset"? I'll put this into perspective for you. If you are fortunate enough to live to be 100 years old, you will have lived for over 876,000 hours. Considering an average of eight hours of sleep per night, you'll have been awake for roughly 584,000 hours. And when you factor in your current age, the remaining hours become even fewer!

Now think about this: If you make $40,000 per year over a 40-year career, you will make $1,600,000. Meanwhile, the richest people in the world have net worths in the hundreds of billions of dollars, and the circulation of money in the world is in the trillions.

The point is the supply of money has no limits and can always be increased, whereas the supply of time is extremely limited and can never be increased.

You will always have opportunities to make more money, even if you spend it or lose it. But time spent or lost can never be made again. This is why time, and not money, is your most valuable asset.

Time is also the greatest equalizer in life. Regardless of your status, where you live, who you are, or how much money you have, everyone wakes up with the same amount of time, 24 hours each day. That's why those that invest their time strategically are more successful than those who aimlessly spend it.

Mentally strong people invest their time through "time blocking." Simply put, time blocking prioritizes your goals, enables you to set boundaries, and protects your most valuable asset, time.

When you time block, you become proactive. You have the tools necessary to silence the noise and maintain relentless focus. You commit in advance to activities that are more impactful and rewarding, rather than trying to squeeze them in after what seems to be urgent, but often not as important.

Over the long term, you'll gain an advantage over those who don't time block. Studies have shown that a week that is time blocked produces significantly more productivity than an unstructured week. Said differently, those who time block produce the same amount of productivity in significantly less time.

Stephen Covey, the author of *The 7 Habits of Highly Effective People*, writes in his book that the single best phrase that captures effective time management is to:

"Organize and execute around priorities."

This is the essence of time blocking. It's a three-step process that synthesizes your long-, medium-, and short-term goals.

First, determine your personal mission statement and your purpose (i.e., what you completed in the chapter, "Find Your Purpose"). This defines your *priorities* and sets your long-term goals.

Then, each week, identify three to five of the most important things you want to accomplish that support the purpose you just defined. This *organizes* your key priorities for the week and sets your medium-term goals.

It's important to limit the number of your weekly goals. Otherwise, your focus and energy will be spread too thin, which will lead to stress, frustration, and ultimately, a lack of accomplishment.

Sundar Pichai, the CEO of Alphabet and Google, who probably has one of the busiest and most demanding schedules, has said:

> *"At the beginning of every week, I plan three to five things I want to accomplish, and focus on those only."*

Finally, each day, allocate your time into ten separate blocks to help you achieve your weekly goals. This is the *execution* which ensures that how you invest your time is synthesized with your medium- and long-term goals. The ten blocks are:

1. **"Sleep"**: Time to replenish brain function as discussed in the chapter, "Take Care of Your Grass."
2. **"Exercise"**: Activities to maintain or improve physical health.
3. **"Relationships"**: Time to build and maintain personal and professional relationships. Personal relationships include family and friends. Professional relationships include colleagues, clients, and partners.
4. **"Deep Focus"**: An activity that requires mental or physical effort to achieve a goal. Important decisions should also be made during this time. This should be completed when your mind is the freshest. Focus on the

hard tasks during this time. Too often we like doing the easy things because we feel accomplished, but that's not the appropriate use of time for this block. Silence all distractions so you can have relentless focus.

5. **"Learn"**: Time to acquire a new understanding, knowledge, or skill to promote personal growth and development. Associate this with "the 8% Goal" as discussed in the chapter, "Take Care of Your Grass."

6. **"Think"**: Time to let your mind wander, which is a form of mindfulness. Often your most creative thoughts come when you provide your mind the opportunity to wander. This is also time for planning your weekly goals and reflecting on past accomplishments, failures, and experiences. This block can occur in various forms such as walking, showering, driving, and meditating.

7. **"Other Work"**: Time for delegation training or administrative tasks such as checking email, doing household chores, checking social media, and doing the easy, non-urgent, unimportant tasks, both personal and professional. *Do not do these tasks during your peak mental performance times.* Save that mental energy for your Deep Focus block.

8. **"Play"**: Time for entertainment, fun, and recreation. During this block, you should do whatever makes you happy; this promotes a sense of well-being and makes life worth living.

9. **"Rest"**: Time to relax, stop working or moving, refresh, and regain strength. If you feel like you are hitting a wall emotionally, remember that sometimes walls are there so

you can lean on them and rest. It's okay to take extended breaks and rest. Everyone needs it.

10. **"Leakage"**: Time that is lost or used between daily activities. It allows you to be imperfect. Leakage includes the transition time between blocks, such as getting up in the morning, taking short breaks, eating, going to the bathroom, showering, getting ready, interruptions, and distractions. Remember, perfection is not attainable. You will always have leakage. The key is to try and minimize it.

A common misconception about time blocking is that it involves doing things at the same time each day. That is just not sustainable in the long run because life gets in the way. If you are too rigid with specific times, you become inflexible, which impacts your ability to develop quality relationships and enjoy life's spontaneous moments.

A person who exhibits the traits of the Posimistiq Mind, time blocks in cumulative hours (e.g., two hours), not specific times (e.g., 9:00 a.m.-11:00 a.m.). In other words, they allow themselves to invest their time in their blocks at different times each day. It's no different than a person having their coffee at 7:00 a.m. one day and at 7:30 a.m. the next day. The goal is still accomplished, regardless of the specific time.

This is why it's important to think of time blocking as a three-step process that *organizes* and *executes* around your *priorities* (i.e., synthesizing your long-, medium-, and short-term goals), and to think in cumulative hours, not specific times during the day. Doing this allows you to remain flexible each day and hold yourself accountable to more achievable expectations as life happens in real-time. Think of the three-step process as a means to an end, but do not let it dictate your minute-by-minute schedule or make you lose sight of what is most important. As Covey writes in his book:

"Your planning tool should be your servant, never your master."

It's now time for you to start thinking of time as your currency. Remember, an investment in time pays the most interest. The longer you invest, the greater your returns will be. If you only have 24 hours in the day, how do you want to invest your time? The following are key points to remember before you begin.

- Your investment strategy is never final. As you grow, learn, reflect, and evolve, your daily investment strategy should evolve with you to remain synthesized with your weekly and long-term priorities.
- Target three different types of "days" for your week, not just one. These include relentless focus, ½ MTO (mental time off), and full MTO. In the chapter, "Take Care of Your Grass," we will delve into the concept of MTO. However, in simple terms, MTO days include more time dedicated to rest and play, instead of relentless focus. Taking mental days off is crucial to ensure optimal mental performance over an extended period.
- The amount of time you allocate to each block is unique to you and based on your purpose and goals. For example,

if your priority is to get in shape, then your block of time that is dedicated to exercising will be longer than someone who has other goals.

- Larger blocks do not need to be completed in consecutive hours. For example, if your investment strategy is to have four hours of deep focus in a day, it can be accomplished in two separate two-hour blocks.
- You will never achieve 100% of your plan every single day. It is just not sustainable in the long run, so don't set that unrealistic expectation for yourself. Instead, think of daily time blocking as your *compass* that will keep you pointed in the right direction, toward your weekly goals and long-term purpose, and do your best to follow it.

No matter how you decide to block your time, keep the following priorities in mind:

1. Your highest priorities should be "self-care" activities such as sleep, exercise, and nutrition. These help you cope with the demands and stress of daily life. If you can't take care of yourself, how do you expect to accomplish anything else? Remember, self-care is not selfish. Taking care of yourself allows you to give more to others.
2. Your second highest priority should be relationships. Having strong, deep relationships contributes to higher levels of happiness. Additionally, success is not always about what you know, but about who you know. Successful people spend time building and preserving relationships.

3. Deep focus should be your third highest priority. A majority of progress and success in life is achieved through the work accomplished during this block.

4. Learning should be your fourth highest priority. We will dive into the importance of this in the chapter, "Take Care of Your Grass."

5. Each day must have a sufficient allocation of sleep and leakage because they are not 100% avoidable. We will discuss how you can minimize leakage in the next section.

6.

Three-Step Time Block Worksheet

Priorities (long term; your purpose)	
What are you good at?	
What brings you joy?	
What breaks your heart?	
Organize (medium term)	
Weekly goal one	
Weekly goal two	
Weekly goal three	
Weekly goal four	
Weekly goal five	

	Execute (short term)		
Investment hours per day	Relentless focus	½ MTO	Full MTO
Sleep	[e.g., 8 hours]		
Exercise			
Relationships			
Deep Focus			
Learn			
Think			
Other Work			

		Play			
		Rest			
		Leakage			
		Total hours*			

*Make sure the total hours in each column add up to 24 hours.

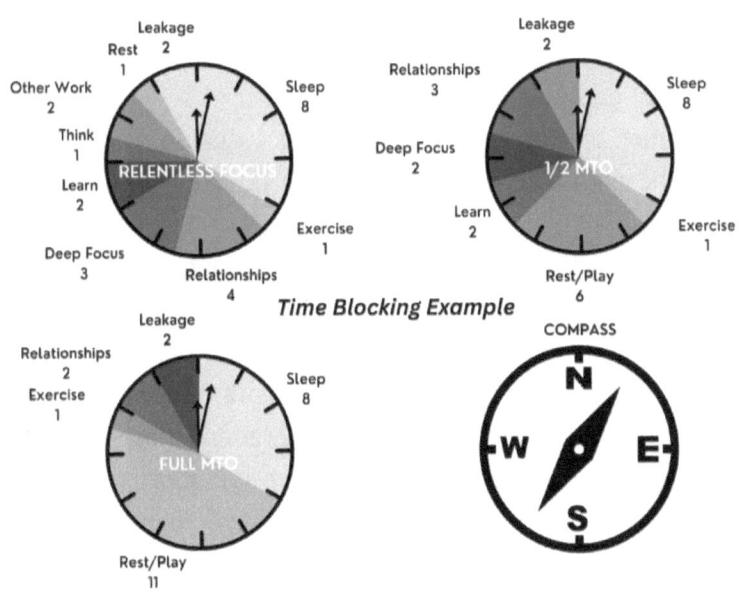

Time Blocking Example

Buy

While it's not literally possible to buy time, mentally strong and successful people maximize time within their day (through effective time management) and minimize their leakage. They silence even the smallest sounds of noise with the following four techniques:

1. Budget money to save time.
2. Eliminate distractions.
3. Delegate.
4. Declutter by saying "no."

Budget money to save time: "Having money makes you rich, but having time makes you wealthy." This expression has been repeated many times by business leaders, philosophers, and other successful people.

In other words, time is your most valuable asset, so when given the choice, you should choose time over money, every time.

However, too often people do the opposite. They spend significant time saving a couple of bucks. Examples include driving long distances to find the best deal, comparison shopping, coupon clipping, staying on the phone with customer service for hours to get a small refund, taking connecting flights, and completing do-it-yourself projects when it is more time efficient to hire someone else or purchase a product that's already put together.

While these actions may seem like money-saving tactics, they can end up being time-consuming and ultimately not worth the effort. For example, let's say you spend four hours scouring the internet for the best deal, driving to multiple stores, and haggling with sales associates to save $25. While you may feel like you've accomplished something, the reality is that you've only earned an equivalent of $6.25 per hour, when you likely could have spent those four hours doing something more productive or even making more money. To determine whether the money you are saving from your efforts is worth it or not, you can use a simple rule of thumb: *If the hourly rate is lower than what you would accept for a professional job, then it's not a worthwhile, money-saving tactic.*

Now, if these activities bring you joy, then that is a reason to do them as part of your play or rest blocks. But deciding just to save money when it does not make or break your budget, without factoring in the opportunity cost of lost time, is not a productive mindset. Weak-minded people choose to save money over time despite marginal returns, even though they have the opportunity, skill set, or awareness to spend time on activities that are more financially productive or beneficial for their mental health.

The strongest-minded and successful people choose to *spend money* to *save time*. This is the winning trade for successful people because they use the time saved and allocate it toward other, more productive areas that are aligned with their mission, purpose, and values.

The challenge we all face is that it is human instinct to choose money over time. This is because money is tangible, and time is not. Money can be used to pay for our most critical survival needs, and time cannot. But this way of thinking can create noise and distract us from things that truly lead to a fulfilling and successful life. This is the mental hurdle you must overcome to build mental strength.

The technique to get over this mental hurdle is to categorize time-saving purchases as an expense in your budget. Just as you budget and spend money on food, shelter, clothing, and entertainment, *you must do the same for time-saving purchases and decisions.*

If you're concerned about the cost of time-saving purchases, or if you feel like you can't afford to make them, take a closer look at your personal budget. Start by assessing your spending in terms of "wants" and "needs". As Suze Orman, a personal finance expert, said:

> *"If you want to become financially secure, you need to develop a spending plan that prioritizes your needs over your wants."*

By distinguishing between your "wants" and "needs", you can make smarter decisions about where to allocate your resources and create a budget that allows you to make time-saving purchases.

Needs are essential expenses that are necessary for survival, such as food, housing, and healthcare. These expenses are required to maintain a basic standard of living and cannot be avoided.

Wants, on the other hand, are noise! They are non-essential expenses that are not necessary for survival but provide comfort or enjoyment, such as entertainment, luxury goods, and travel.

When necessary, these expenses can be reduced or eliminated without negatively impacting one's basic needs.

Often, people tend to spend money on *wants*, mistaking them for *needs*. For example, having a home is a *need*, but purchasing an overly extravagant house is a *want*. Basic groceries like fruits and vegetables are a *need*, but gourmet food and dining out are a *want*. Owning a car is usually a *need*, but owning a luxury car is a *want*. For most people, the internet is a *need*, but subscribing to multiple streaming services is a *want*. Basic clothing like shirts, pants, and shoes are *needs*, but luxury clothing and trendy fashion items are *wants*.

To build mental strength, achieve success, and maximize your potential, you must shift your mindset to think of *time-saving purchases* as a *need*, not a *want*. Then begin to reallocate your spending from your *wants* to *time-saving purchases*. While people make all different levels of income, we all have the power to scale back the money we spend on our "wants" and spend that money on time-saving purchases that benefit us instead.

A simple trick to minimize impulsive "want" purchases is to wait for seven days after feeling the urge to buy something. If, after the waiting period, you still desire the item and it fits within your budget, then you can decide to purchase it. Often, you'll find that after a week, many of those wants fade away, and as a result, you'll have some extra money in your budget that you didn't know you had.

To be clear, it's important to be mindful of costs. But there's a difference between saving money efficiently and spending time on things that don't make a meaningful difference. Aside from essential food, water, and shelter, a mentally strong person's highest priority expense is time-saving purchases.

Your current objective should be to identify ways to increase the amount of money you allocate toward time-saving purchases. To get started, use the budget framework below to determine what percentage of your after-tax net income is currently spent on time-saving purchases. Once you define your current spending, consider one time-saving purchase that you don't currently make but could add to your life starting today. For example, consider:

- subscribing to services like Amazon Prime to avoid frequent trips to multiple stores.
- subscribing to meal delivery services that provide pre-cooked meals or meal kits that come with all the necessary ingredients and instructions for faster home cooking.
- hiring professionals to clean your home or maintain your lawn.
- going to a car wash instead of washing your car yourself.
- integrating smart home devices into your living space to automate various tasks, such as the automatic adjustment of your thermostat.
- taking direct flights instead of connecting flights.
- investing in home gym equipment which can save time; compared to going to a gym or fitness studio.
- utilizing ride-sharing services like Uber can be more time-efficient than public transportation.

Next, aim to increase your income allocation from "wants" to time-saving purchases by 1%, and gradually work your way up by 2%, 3%, and so on, finding the right balance that suits your lifestyle.

Personal Budget	% of After-Tax Net Income		
	Current	**Strong Mind**	**Example**
Shelter			20%
Food			5%
Children or other caretaker expenses			20%
Transportation			2%
Time-saving purchases			10%
Financial investments			25%
Emergency funds			10%
"Wants"			8%
Total			**100%**

Note: Shelter costs refer to housing-related expenses, such as mortgage payments, insurance, property taxes, and more. Child costs encompass any expenditure not related to food and shelter involved in raising your children or otherwise providing for your friends and family. Transportation expenses include the cost of vehicles, trains, and other forms of travel. Financial investments encompass short-term, long-term, and retirement investments. Emergency funds are funds set aside to aid during periods of job loss, emergency home repairs, healthcare costs, and unexpected expenses. Lastly, "wants" include non-essential expenses like entertainment, designer clothing, vacations, and so on.

Once you categorize time-saving purchases as another expense in your budget and start associating time-saving purchases as a need, you will become more comfortable making decisions that cost more money to save you more time. You will notice less noise in your life and your days will feel significantly longer, leaving you more time to be more productive and do things you enjoy.

Eliminate distractions: A one-minute check of your emails, text messages, or social media disrupts your focus. Taking a phone call at an inappropriate time disrupts your focus. Constantly alternating between blocks, such as deep focus and other work (i.e., meetings and checking emails), disrupts your focus.

Think of distractions like a needle to a balloon. Just as one needle can pop even the biggest balloon, one distraction can disrupt your entire focus.

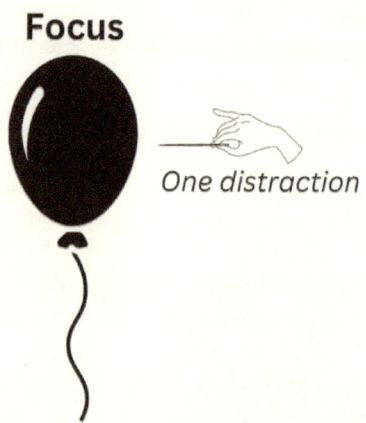

Focus

One distraction

Why? All of these distractions introduce new thoughts into your mind. They tempt you to respond to what you see. You feel pressured to address new or outstanding tasks and responsibilities, which makes it difficult to focus on the original task at hand.

Even more, it takes time and mental effort to refocus on a new task. Some studies suggest that it takes up to 25 minutes to refocus on a task after you get distracted. A one-minute check of your email, phone, and social media can use 1.8% of your time in a day!

Mentally strong and successful people silence this noise. They eliminate distractions to maintain relentless focus and create time within their day.

You've already planned your investment strategy. There is an appropriate time for everything, including looking at your emails, text messages, and social media. Remember, depending on the day, you may only have one or two hours to dedicate to your essential blocks, such as relationships and deep focus. It's vital not to squander this time since it's where most of your success will be created and achieved.

All that's left for you to do is honor your commitment to focus on the block or task at hand, so you can have better, more efficient, and uninterrupted time. Remember the following techniques to silence the noise, minimize leakage, and maximize your time as you live within your blocks:

Do	Don't
Do focus on one task at a time.	*Don't* multitask.
Do batch similar tasks together (e.g., checking emails, voicemails, and text messages).	*Don't* keep switching between tasks in short increments (e.g., sporadically checking emails throughout the day).
Do take control of your calendar.	*Don't* have meetings scheduled intermittently throughout the day. Try to schedule all meetings during your Other Work block.
Do put your phone on Do Not Disturb during your deep focus block.	*Don't* let your phone notifications become a distraction.
Do start your day with mental clarity.	*Don't* start your day with phone notifications. This will derail your mental focus for the day. If it can wait the time you were sleeping, it can wait a little longer.

Delegate: Have you heard the phrase, *"If you want something done right, do it yourself"*? Do you get frustrated when you know you could do something faster and better than someone else, so you end up taking the lead and doing it yourself? We all experience this. Unfortunately, it adds significant noise to our lives.

Consider this, it is often said that the most important position in American football is the quarterback of a football team. The quarterback is responsible for making strategic decisions on the field. But even the quarterback must trust and rely on other players during the game to achieve success. He must trust the offensive lineman to block, the wide receivers to catch, the running backs to run, and the defenders to play defense. He delegates!

Imagine if the quarterback didn't delegate. Imagine if he tried to block for himself, throw to himself, and play defense alone. He would not be able to do it successfully and he would burn out quickly in the process.

Your life is no different. You are the quarterback in your life, but you still need to delegate. *Delegation allows you to leverage the time of others to accomplish the tasks at hand.* When you delegate, you add more hours to your day. Although you start each day with 24 hours, if you delegate a two-hour task to one person, you've just added two more hours to your day.

Delegation creates time for you to prepare and focus on more important activities, especially those aligned with your priorities and weekly goals.

Too often we don't delegate to others because of the significant learning curve involved in the delegation process. In the short term, the learning curve creates the feeling that you are regressing, moving slower, and using more energy trying to teach someone how to do something, than if you just did the task yourself.

But progress in life is not linear. Sometimes you have to take a step down before you can go up. This is the gap that mentally weak people fail to see past.

Effective delegation takes time, effort, and training. The benefits do not occur instantly. But the return on investment is exponential over the long term. A non-delegator may get higher returns in the short term, but over the long term, they will plateau because there is only so much time in a day.

Mentally strong and successful people know the learning curve is part of the delegation process that will ultimately lead to exponential returns. So, they invest time in it.

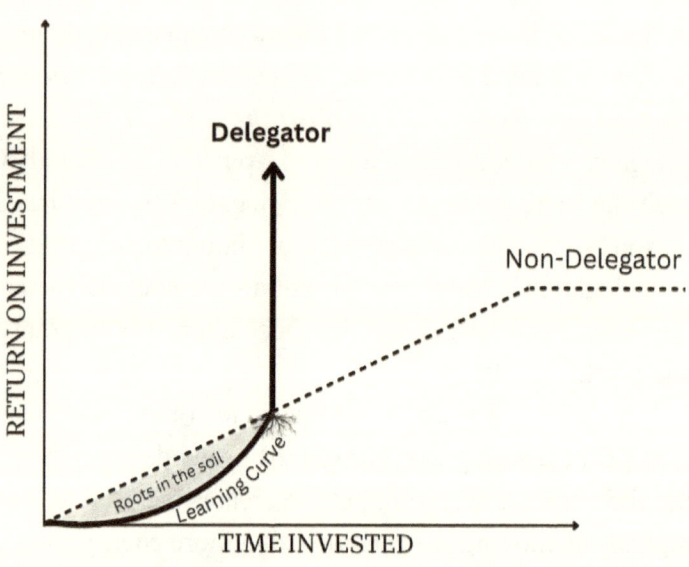

Take, for example, the Sequoia tree. These trees can take several years to grow and develop beneath the surface before they finally emerge from the ground. Once they do, they grow to be over 300 feet tall and have diameters as wide as 30 feet!

Think of the learning curve as the soil beneath the surface. This is where you must nurture the roots of each Sequoia tree. Each person you delegate to is another tree in your forest.

The learning curve is where you must spend time training, clearly communicating the overall objective, and providing constructive feedback as the person develops. This all occurs below the surface.

You will not see results instantly. But over time, incremental progress will occur each day.

Think about parents raising children from newborns to adults. All survival responsibilities of newborns reside with the parents on day one. As children grow into toddlers, pre-teens, adolescents, and adults, more responsibilities are delegated to them. If parents never spent time training and delegating responsibilities to their children, they would still be cleaning their children's bottoms today!

The fatal flaw in effective delegation comes *after* the learning curve. A person might stop delegating because the end results don't live up to that person's standards or are not exactly how that person would have done it.

Recognize that when you delegate, you'll get different results than if you did it yourself. But that doesn't mean the results will be inferior.

The question to consider is not, "*Is that how I would have done it?*" Nothing will ever be done exactly the way you would have done it. When you set this expectation, the fear of losing control and the inability to let go multiplies, and you become unable to delegate and leverage the time of others.

The question to consider is, *"Do the results support the big-picture objective?"* Did the child's bottom get cleaned?

Remember, no Sequoia tree that sprouts from the surface is exactly the same. Instead of producing one perfect tree in the time you have, it's better to produce a forest of hundreds of strong trees in the same amount of time.

Declutter by saying no: Clutter is noise. Visualize your clothes closet at home. The more clothes you put in the closet, the harder it is to remain organized. The more options for you to choose from, the more distracted and overwhelmed you become, and the harder it is to decide what to wear.

Your mental capacity is no different. The more things you say yes to, the more thoughts you allow into your mind, and the more your mind gets filled with clutter.

Mentally strong people declutter their minds to manage their mental capacity. They have a never-ending focus to take stock of their thoughts, feelings, and commitments and let go of those that no longer serve them.

By decluttering and organizing your thoughts, you silence the noise and free up mental space. This creates a sense of calm and energy to focus on more important and meaningful activities.

To declutter, you just have to get comfortable saying no. This means saying no to certain tasks at work, to some activities that you're not interested in, or to events that don't serve you.

But this is easier said than done. Saying no is difficult because we all have a desire to please others. We don't want to disappoint anyone or face confrontation. We might feel guilty, lack the confidence to say no, or have a fear of missing out.

To build mental strength and maximize your full potential, you need to learn to say no. It's important to keep in mind that when you agree to do something you don't truly want to do, you're simultaneously saying no to the things you actually want to do. Everything you say yes to and allow into your mind is more noise that can distract you from achieving what you truly desire. Steve Jobs once said:

"You have to say no to the good ideas, so you can focus on the great ideas."

It is possible to learn how to say no more effectively. You just have to practice. Start small in lower-pressure situations to get comfortable using the word and setting boundaries. While you can also provide your reasons for saying no, don't feel the need to. Something as simple as "I'm sorry, but I'm going to have to decline" is all you need. Even if someone asks why, the difference between a mentally strong and weak mind is recognizing you do not need to give a reason.

One effective way to say no without overexplaining is to follow a simple three-step formula. *This involves starting with an expression of gratitude, followed by a clear statement of refusal, and ending with good wishes.* For example, you could say, "Thank you for considering me (gratitude), but I'm not able to do it at the moment (refusal). Let me know how it turns out (good wishes)." Or you could say, "I really appreciate you thinking of me (gratitude), but I won't be able to attend the event (refusal).

Have a great time and keep me updated (good wishes)." No matter what you include in the three-step formula, it's important to use a tone that is firm and direct while also being kind, respectful, and compassionate.

Learning how to confidently say no is the essential skill in effective decision-making to silence the noise. The only thing left for you to do is learn how to confidently *decide* what to say no to.

Decide

There is a big difference between what you feel needs to be done and what actually needs to be done. Knowing what really matters will help you make decisions to maximize the use of your time, decrease your stress, and achieve success.

Making decisions involves tradeoffs. Having tradeoffs creates noise. Given the limited time in a day, tradeoffs are a normal part of life and involve compromise. *When you say yes to one thing, it means you are saying no to everything else in that moment.*

Understanding tradeoffs that can maximize your success can be challenging because it sometimes requires you to consider multiple conflicting goals. This creates more noise which makes it hard to make a decision that feels satisfactory, or even decide at all. This is known as "analysis paralysis," the state of overanalyzing a situation to the point where it becomes difficult to decide.

But if I simply gave you the option to trade me an asset with a lower value for an asset with a higher value, wouldn't you do it every time?

This is how mentally strong and successful people think to silence the noise that can interfere with fast, decisive decision-making. They follow the Matrix of Importance and Urgency to help make winning decisions.

The Matrix of Importance and Urgency: Five-star General of World War II and the 34th President of the United States, Dwight Eisenhower, who was famous for his effective time management skills, is often credited with developing the "Matrix of Importance and Urgency," also known as the "Eisenhower Matrix."

The idea of the Matrix is that everything should be evaluated based on its level of *importance* and *urgency* and then prioritized accordingly.

In the context of decision-making, urgency means reactive. It requires immediate attention and is time sensitive. Importance is proactive. It requires your utmost attention, but it's not necessarily time sensitive.

Mentally strong people associate the word important with their long-term purpose, mission, values, and goals, and they associate the word urgent with something that will result in significant consequences if it is not addressed quickly. Stephen Covey dissects the Matrix further in his book, stating:

> *"Urgent matters are usually visible. They press on us; they insist on action. They're often popular with others. They're usually right in front of us. And often they are pleasant, easy, fun to do. But so often they are unimportant!*

"Importance, on the other hand, has to do with results. If something is important, it contributes to your mission, your values, your high-priority goals."

Ultimately, the Matrix empowers you to invest your time in one of four ways: Deciding between things that are "important and urgent," "important and not urgent," "not important and urgent," and "not important and not urgent." For example:

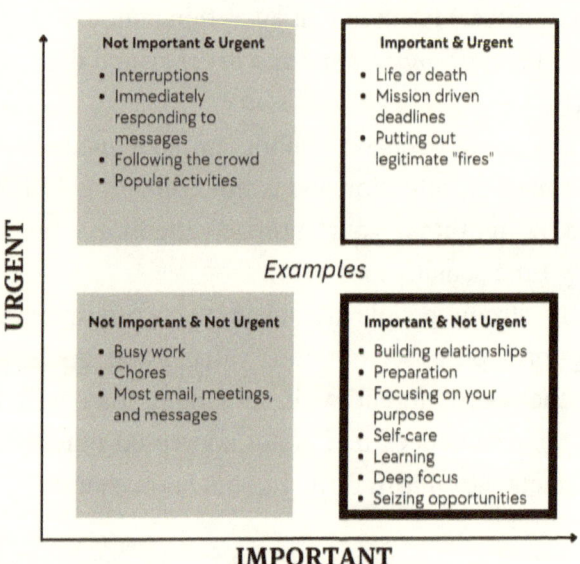

Examples

Silencing the noise requires you to allocate your time investment in each quadrant effectively. The strategy mentally strong people use when deciding between tradeoffs is to associate the time invested in each section with the following words:

1. *"Prioritized efficiency"* = important and urgent
2. *"Maximize"* = important and not urgent
3. *"Delay"* = not important and urgent
4. *"Eliminate"* = not important and not urgent

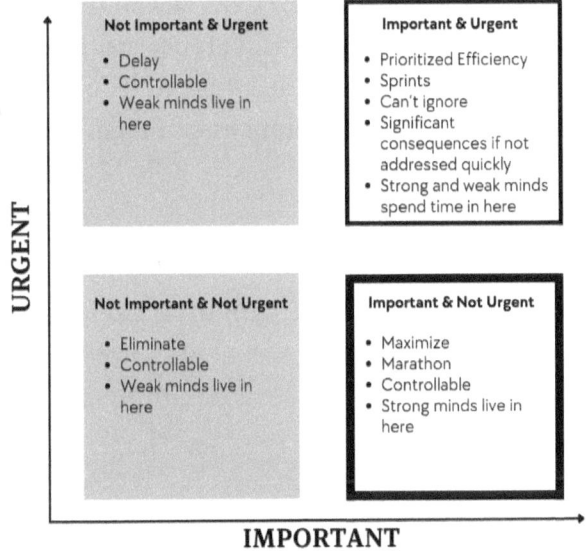

Remember these two points:

1. Not all urgent tasks are important, and not all important tasks are urgent.
2. There is a difference between what takes *priority* and where you should spend the *most time*.

Things that are "important and urgent" should take the highest *priority*, but they don't come up that often. Over the course of your life, you should spend the most amount of *time* on things that are actually "important and *not* urgent."

To put this into perspective, visualize a weight scale. On one side of the scale, picture the important and not urgent tasks, where more time is invested. As more time is invested, the clock becomes larger and heavier. On the other side of the scale, picture the few things that are important and urgent that are much more infrequent. Because less time is spent here, the clock is smaller and lighter. Also, notice how unimportant things aren't even on the scale.

Time Scale

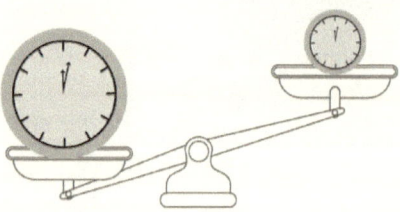

Important & Urgent
LESS TIME

Important & Not Urgent
MAXIMIZE TIME

Something that is "important and urgent" might be if your house is on fire or if someone is hurt or dying. Of course, these things are important and require immediate attention. But you wouldn't spend most of your time addressing these things, as they aren't that frequent.

In contrast, things that are "important and not urgent" might include studying and working toward your degree, learning the ropes of your new job, getting into shape, or working on building or repairing relationships. All of these things are important, but they're not necessarily urgent. If you miss one day of working toward these goals while you focus on other tasks at hand, you probably won't fall behind. But in the aggregate, you'll still want to devote most of your time toward these goals.

Important and not urgent: Think of your life as a marathon, not a sprint. You spend significantly more time running a marathon, than you do in a sprint. But the end result is you end up running much further in a marathon.

A marathon requires endurance, persistence, and patience. Sprints require immediate and quick action. They require urgency. Urgency is, more or less, absent in a marathon. If you become urgent in a marathon and constantly sprint, you will burn out and not finish.

During a marathon, you'll encounter obstacles or distractions that require you to make decisions. For example, you'll have to decide whether to take a break and rest or continue to push forward. Each decision takes up time and directly impacts when you will finish the race.

Your life is no different. As you run life's marathon, you will encounter distractions that require you to make decisions, such as whether to check your phone for the latest email or maintain your deep focus block.

Mentally strong people stay focused on their goals and make winning decisions that keep them on track during their marathons. They live most of their lives on the track, not off it. And it is where you should maximize the amount of time you spend in your life to go as far as you are capable of.

The course of your marathon is made up of your mission, purpose, values, and goals. It is the priorities you defined in the "Long-Term Priorities" section of the Three-Step Time Block Worksheet. These are the things that are important, but not necessarily urgent, such as planning, preparing, focusing, building relationships, practicing self-care, deep focus, and seizing opportunities that are aligned with your purpose as they are presented.

If you miss one on a given day, there won't be significant consequences. But they are extremely important, because to achieve what you already defined as success, it requires sustained effort and discipline over a longer period of time. It requires you to stay on track. Anything in life worth having takes time.

As you run your marathon, it's essential to monitor your "splits." Splits are the short-term sections of the race that marathon runners track to gauge their progress. If you run too fast during your splits, you will burn out and not finish the race. But if you don't keep pace, you will fall behind. The three to five weekly goals that you defined in the Three-Step Time Block Worksheet are the "splits" in your marathon. It's important to define these weekly and monitor your progress. Limiting it to three to five goals will give you your pace and help you finish the marathon.

By thinking of your life as a marathon, you have the tools necessary to silence the noise and overcome obstacles and distractions. To finish your marathon, you need to stay on course. You need to invest significant time in your priorities that are important but not necessarily urgent, rather than get thrown off course by urgent or short-term distractions.

Staying on course requires you to make decisions. The next time you need to decide how to invest your time, ask yourself if the distraction in front of you is part of your marathon's course. If it's not, then say no to it. Otherwise, you'll make it much harder on yourself to get to the finish line or never get there at all.

Important and urgent: Regardless of who you are, there will be brief times in your life where it is appropriate to think of that time period as a sprint. This occurs when something is truly important and urgent.

The fatal flaw in being able to silence the noise is sprinting too often because you do not understand what is actually important *and* urgent. If you are constantly sprinting, you won't be able to finish the marathon.

Things that are truly important and urgent are things you cannot ignore and which you must sprint to. *The key here is recognizing there are very few things in life that are important and urgent.*

For something to be considered important and urgent, there must be a significant consequence if it is not dealt with promptly. The slower you work through it, the more detrimental the consequences will be.

This is why "prioritized efficiency" (*not* "maximize") are the keywords associated with "important and urgent." Important and urgent tasks should receive the highest priority but without a lot of time or frequency spent on these tasks. You sprint to things that are truly important and urgent and address them immediately.

For example, it's important *and* urgent if your house is on fire. You'll sprint to put the fire out or call the fire department. If someone is hurt or dying, that is important and urgent, and you'll sprint to help them or call 911.

But if something can be delayed without significant consequence, then it is not urgent. If your boss calls you when you're in the middle of finishing a work-related task, it may be important, but it is not necessarily urgent. Ultimately, most bosses would rather have their employees focus and complete tasks than jump around from one to another. You might just have to explain what you were doing and why you were unavailable to manage expectations going forward.

Too often, mentally weak people associate things that seem to be urgent as also being important. This is because when things are sitting right in front of us and insisting action, it creates a sense of urgency. In reality, though, those things that seem to be urgent can wait.

Do not let these distractions disrupt your relentless focus or set your schedule for the day. You need to say no to these distractions so you can spend the most time focusing on your true priorities, your marathon. If you are constantly sprinting, it will lead to burnout.

The next time you are faced with a distraction, ask yourself, "What is the most significant consequence if I don't address this for another hour, another day, or another week? What if I never address it at all? How will my life be impacted?"

If the answer isn't a loss of life, loss of your home, or loss of your job, then it's probably not important *and* urgent. It can wait. Over time, if you keep delaying or avoiding these distractions, you will learn that most of them truly never needed to be addressed in the first place. They really weren't important. Think about all the time you just saved yourself in this scenario. This is the key decision-making technique to silence the noise that distracts you most often.

"Not important and urgent" and "not important and not urgent": In a marathon, you will encounter countless distractions that are not important. These could be distractions from spectators and other runners, your own negative thoughts and emotions, small details such as changes in terrain or weather, or comparing yourself to other runners. Successful runners stay focused on the big picture, which is keeping pace and finishing the marathon. They do not get distracted by unimportant things.

Your life is no different. Unimportant distractions are everywhere. They include busy work, mundane chores, most emails, messages, and meetings (especially those that are not urgent), interrupting tasks, spending too much time on social media, engaging in gossip, following the crowd, and worrying about things beyond your control.

If I simply asked you, "Do you want to do something that is not important?" your answer would be no.

However, weak-minded people don't consider this question before acting. Instead, they react to what's in front of them as being important. As a result, they spend too much time being distracted by things that don't really matter. They end up living most of their lives in the quadrants designated as "not important," the same quadrants that mentally strong people delay or ignore completely.

Consider the tasks involved with moving into a new home. You have a list of things you must or should do, such as obtaining homeowners' insurance, setting up your weekly trash pickup, changing the locks, and installing internet access. But oftentimes, people have another list of things they want to accomplish once they move into their new home, such as painting the walls, hanging pictures, updating light fixtures, or replacing the flooring.

Many new homeowners think these tasks are important and urgent. But most of these tasks are not urgent whatsoever, and may not even be important. For example, if new homeowners hate the color blue, it's probably important for them to paint over their blue walls so they can enjoy their home and be in a positive mental state. On the other hand, while those same homeowners might want to install new carpets to ensure that the house is clean, they can simply hire a cleaning service to clean their rugs, which takes significantly less time and money to accomplish.

In fact, it's often said that if you wait a year after moving into a new home, you'll decide not to do most of the things on your original decorative to-do list. As time passes and you create memories in the house and get to the point where your new house feels like a home, the initial urgency and importance of these tasks often fade away. In other words, the tasks that you initially thought were important and urgent often turn out to be neither.

The next time you are faced with a distraction and have a decision to make, pause. Take a moment to consider whether it's actually important. Important is defined as something supporting your purpose, mission, values, and goals. Remember what's important to you may not be important to someone else. Ask yourself if this task will matter in one month. If it won't, let it go.

When you say no to things that are not important and don't serve your purpose, you create time in your schedule and space in your mind to focus on your true priorities.

Deadline fallacy: It's easy to say no to things that are not important and not urgent. But one of the hardest things to do is say no to things that are perceived to be urgent because we incorrectly assume they are important.

Deadlines create a sense of urgency. Urgency creates a sense of false importance. The trick is to not let deadlines create a sense of false importance.

To make my point, Chris Voss, former FBI hostage negotiator and author of the book, *Never Split the Difference: Negotiating as if Your Life Depended on It,* states in the book:

> *"Deadlines are almost never ironclad. Deadlines are often arbitrary, almost always flexible, and hardly ever trigger the consequences we think—or are told—they will. Deadlines regularly make people do impulsive things that*

are against their best interests, because we all
have a natural tendency to fear deadlines."

The point is to always take the time that you need to make the best decision for yourself. Don't let deadlines influence your decision-making process. Most deadlines are flexible and arbitrary, including deadlines set by external sources or internal pressures you create. They can usually be delayed.

Take, for example, a litigator who receives a nasty email from an opposing attorney on the opposite side of the case. The opposing attorney tells the litigator to produce certain documents and sets a one-week "deadline" for the litigator to do so. The opposing attorney says that if the documents aren't received within a week, he will run to court, take back a settlement offer, make things even harder for the litigator, or have another negative consequence.

It's natural to fear the consequences of missing a deadline. But as Chris Voss states in his book, deadlines can make people act impulsively instead of holding their ground. And as seen in the example above, the opposing attorney's "deadline" is completely arbitrary. There is usually room for flexibility – whether it be a day, a week, or a month – to consider whether you want or even need to complete the task at hand. Despite the opposing attorney's "deadline," the litigator should first consider whether she is obligated to produce the documents in the first place, instead of acting impulsively for fear of the consequences of missing the opposing attorney's deadline.

Procrastination is a useful skill when used in the right moments. The moment to use it is when things are urgent and not important.

Life is a constant negotiation. When you are making decisions, you are actually negotiating with yourself. When you are faced with something that seems urgent, but cannot associate it with something important (i.e., your purpose, mission, values, and goals), can you delay addressing it? What's the most significant consequence if you miss the deadline? This technique of procrastinating a task to silence the noise will lead to one of two outcomes:

1. At some point, the distraction will turn into something that you can justify as supporting your mission, purpose, and goals. It is then that you can invest time in it.
2. After the dust settles, the level of urgency will begin to disappear. You will notice the thing that seemed so urgent a couple of weeks ago never needed to be done at all.

Ultimately, prioritizing tasks based on importance and urgency, rather than reacting to every distraction, is how mentally strong people silence the noise to make the best decisions.

Things that are truly important and urgent have significant consequences if they're not addressed quickly. You sprint to these because you do not have a choice. But you can't sprint your whole life. Instead, run through things that are important. Spend the most time *running* your marathon, which is your mission, purpose, values, and goals. Anything else that is not important should be delayed, eliminated, or delegated to others.

The only thing left for you to do is practice everything you just learned. Everything you learned in this chapter is about progress, not perfection. The outcomes of your decisions will never be 100% perfect. Do not get discouraged in the short term if some of your decisions end up being the wrong decisions. Discouragement is noise.

Do not let uncertainty paralyze your ability to decide. It's okay to live in the unknown. Remember that most decisions can always be reversed. In fact, the faster it can be reversed, the faster you should decide. Paralysis by analysis is noise.

Silence all the noise by reminding yourself that it's often better to take action and learn from any mistakes than to remain stuck in the decision-making process. Executing this decision-making strategy over the long term will lead to mental strength, happiness, and success.

Before we end the chapter, I will leave you with one final challenge: What is one thing you could do in your personal or professional life that, if you did it on a regular basis, would significantly silence the noise in your life?

"For 42 years, I've been making small, regular deposits in this bank of experience, education, and training. And on January 15, 2009, the balance was sufficient so that I could make a large withdrawal."

-Captain Sully

TRAIT 4

DEVELOP RESILIENCE AND PERSEVERANCE

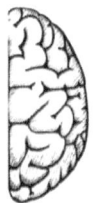

Picture this: You are preparing to take an exam in school. You've attended every class, taken detailed notes, and stayed up every night for the last week studying. You feel you are ready.

It's now the day of the big exam. During the exam, a wave of panic sets in as you look at each question. You realize you don't know the answers to most of the questions. As time ticks away, you are left with no choice but to take your best guesses and hand in your exam.

A couple of days pass and the exam results are ready. Your teacher, at her desk, calls your classmates up one by one and hands them their tests. You notice every person is smiling as they walk back to their desks. You begin to sweat, first slightly, but then more and more as you see more smiles. You anticipate the inevitable is about to happen.

The teacher finally calls out your name. As you slowly walk up to her desk, you notice a stern look on her face. She hands you your grade. In big red font at the top of the page is a giant letter "F." Your heart sinks. As you walk back to your desk, you hear your friend across the room ask, "How did you do?"

Can you relate to this story? If not, then visualize yourself in a scenario where you experienced your biggest failure or setback, where you didn't meet the expectations of yourself, your family, or those closest to you.

Do you recall if you were proud or embarrassed? Encouraged or discouraged? Happy or sad? Most likely, it is the latter of the three questions.

This is the flaw in the circumstances of our mental development. Through the direct or indirect feedback we receive from our guardians, teachers, coaches, or peers, we are taught to think that failure is bad from the moment we enter this world. When you do something incorrectly, break something, or fail, you get in trouble, get yelled at, get grounded, or are told, "Don't do that again!"

Take education, for example. The lowest letter grade you can receive is an F, which represents failure. We are programmed to think there is nothing worse than failure. In other words, anything else you do is better than an F and better than failure.

The repercussions in school get worse and worse as multiple failures occur over time. If you fail one test, you have time to recover. But if you fail two, three, four…ten tests, then you will be held back in school, unable to get into the top universities, and unable to get a prestigious job. From a very young age, we're programmed to think that the more you fail, the worse it is. This causes us to naturally fear failure and try to avoid it.

The truth is, everyone fails in life at one point or another, including mentally strong and successful people. People don't fail just once. They fail multiple times, usually every day.

But mentally strong people recognize there is no success without setbacks and no progress without pitfalls. Failures and setbacks are opportunities for growth and success. It's all part of the success process. There are countless examples of individuals who have turned failure into success. Consider the following individuals:

- Abraham Lincoln lost multiple elections before being elected the 16th President of the United States.
- J.K. Rowling, the author of the *Harry Potter* series, received multiple rejections from publishers before her book was finally accepted.
- Steven Spielberg was rejected from theater, film, and television schools before becoming one of the most successful directors of all time.
- Michael Jordan was cut from his high school varsity basketball team because he was not skilled enough before becoming one of the greatest basketball players of all time.
- Oprah Winfrey was demoted from her job as a news anchor because she was deemed unfit for television before becoming one of the world's most successful television talk show hosts.
- Walt Disney was fired from a newspaper for not being creative enough before creating the Walt Disney Company.

The common theme in all these examples is that these people did not quit after their initial setbacks. They learned from their failures and persevered. They went on to be some of the most successful individuals in history.

Are you starting to see how much you might be leaving on the table when you fear failure, stop trying, and give up too soon?

These examples and countless other studies have shown there is one characteristic that emerges as a significant predictor of success. It's not how smart you are or what your IQ is. It's not your background, genes, family income, or circumstances. And it's not your talent level or luck.

The number one predictor of success is developing the mental strength traits of resilience and perseverance.

The combination of resilience and perseverance is the ability to keep getting back up after you are knocked down, the ability to stay in the fight, and the will to not give up.

However, developing resilience and perseverance is a process. It is not something that can be achieved instantly. It requires time, effort, and the right mindset. The mindset requires you to:

1. recognize that success is not linear; it's scattered, and
2. think like a mountain climber.

By ingraining these techniques into your mindset, you will begin to develop true resilience and perseverance. You will find yourself better equipped to bounce back from any setbacks you encounter. Ultimately, you will find yourself emerging from the setbacks stronger and more resilient than ever before.

Success is not linear; it's scattered

Once upon a time, there were two young men named Paul and Ned. Both always dreamed of becoming successful businessmen.

Paul and Ned worked hard in school to earn degrees in business. Both landed jobs at prestigious companies, and both were quickly promoted within their companies. Everything seemed to be going according to their plans.

As time went on, Paul and Ned encountered obstacles in their careers. Both lost major clients and struggled to add new clients. Paul and Ned both ended up getting demoted.

At this point, Ned was devastated and began to doubt himself. He thought his journey to success was supposed to be a straight line. He became bitter. He blamed others for his misfortune, became disengaged, and lost motivation. He became pessimistic about all opportunities, assuming they would result in failures and setbacks.

However, Paul still believed in himself. He remembered reading a book that taught him that success is not linear. It is a scattered path with twists, turns, ups, and downs.

With this in mind, Paul decided to visualize his failures as stepping stones, each one representing a specific failure that provided him an opportunity to learn and grow.

He began to realize that failure was not something to be feared. He owned his mistakes, worked to get better, and remained optimistic about opportunities that came his way.

As he progressed from stone to stone, learning valuable lessons from each failure, Paul began to see his progress. He noticed each stone was getting bigger and more stable, representing his growing resilience and perseverance.

Over time, Paul and Ned ended up in different spots. Paul regained more customers each year. He was promoted multiple times, eventually to CEO, leading the company to years of success. He was forever known as Posimistiq Paul, hopping from stone to stone, always learning and growing from his failures.

Ned spent years job hopping, looking for the path of least resistance. Ned quit every time he faced a setback. Ultimately, he never progressed further in his career. He was forever known as Negamistiq Ned, the man who was always negative and pessimistic.

The story of Posimistiq Paul and Negamistiq Ned reminds us that success is not a destination with a straight path. Success is a journey, scattered with obstacles that can either knock you down or make you stronger and more resilient.

To truly achieve success, you must be willing to embrace the scattered path. You must not let obstacles and failures defeat you. Instead, you must visualize them as stepping stones on your journey to success.

The most powerful thing you can take away from this chapter is to ingrain the following two visuals in your head:

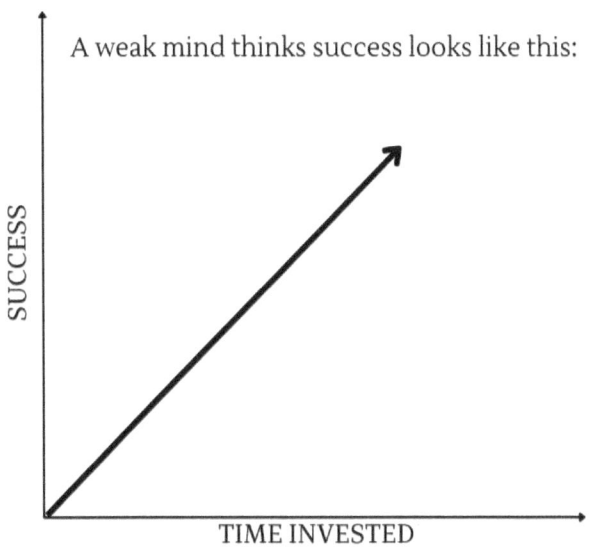

A weak mind thinks success looks like this:

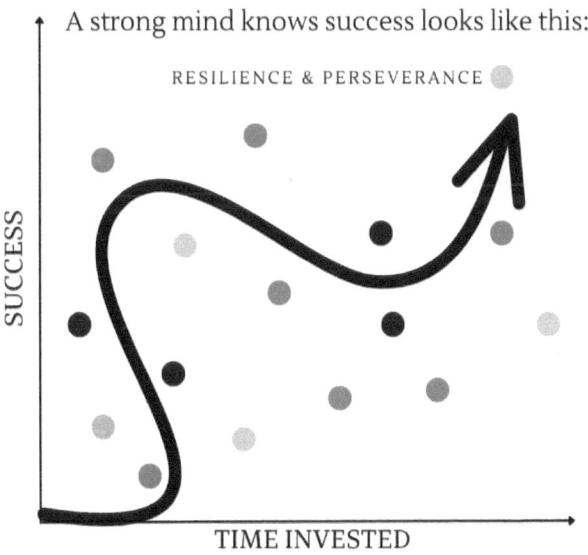

A strong mind knows success looks like this:

RESILIENCE & PERSEVERANCE

The next time you are faced with an obstacle and feel like you got knocked down or off your path, these two visuals will remind you that you are on the right path. You just need to keep hopping from stone to stone. This mindset will help you develop resilience and perseverance.

Be happy with failure: It's easy to be afraid of failure. But it's important to remember that failure is not the end of a journey. It's not a reflection of your self-worth, and it does not mean you are further from success.

Failure is an inevitable part of the journey to success. It's an opportunity for you to learn, adjust, improve, and grow, which brings you one step closer to success. Consider this comment that has been repeated many times by many successful people:

> *"You can either get bitter or better, it's that simple. You either take what has been dealt to you and allow it to make you a better person, or you allow it to tear you down. The choice does not belong to fate; it belongs to you."*

Mentally strong and successful people understand this. They seek failure instead of hiding from it. For example:

- Kobe Bryant, one of the greatest basketball players of all time, not only accepted failure as part of the process but actively sought it out. He stated, *"I like to fail, I like to lose because it teaches me how I can get better and ultimately succeed."*

- Sundar Pichai, CEO of Alphabet and Google, has said, *"If you don't fail sometimes, you are not being ambitious enough. When you are ambitious you might fail a few times, but that's okay because you end up doing something worthwhile which you learn a great deal from."*

- Robert Herjavec, a successful entrepreneur and author, has emphasized that to truly reach your potential, you must get comfortable with failure and continuously push yourself to grow.

- Sara Blakely, the founder of Spanx, attributes part of her success to her father's approach to failure:

"We would come home, sit at the dinner table and my Dad would ask, 'What did you fail at this week?' If I didn't have something to tell him, he would actually be disappointed in me.

"Then there were times I came home and said 'Dad, I tried out for this, and I was horrible,' and he would give me a high five and say, 'Way to go!' At the time it was so confusing, but now I realize he was redefining failure for me. Failure for me didn't become about the outcome, it became about not trying."

Eventually, this mindset enabled her to create Spanx, a billion-dollar company in an industry she had no prior experience, which made her the youngest self-made female billionaire at the time.

It's important to remind yourself that the relationship between success and failure is the opposite of what you learned in school. In school, you were taught that the more you failed, the less successful you would be. However, in life, the more you fail, the closer you get to success.

So, shift your perspective on failure. Instead of fearing it, embrace it as a natural part of the success process. When you do fail, which is inevitable, see it as evidence that you took action and made an effort toward your goal. The only real failure in life is giving up or not even trying in the first place. Consider this comment from Robert Kiyosaki, author of *Rich Dad Poor Dad*:

> *"Winners are not afraid of losing, but losers are. Failure is a part of the process of success. People who avoid failure also avoid success."*

Once you recognize that failures are the stepping stones on your scattered path to success, you will be more motivated to persevere through challenges and learn from your failures. You will develop more resilience and perseverance, which increases your ability to reach your full potential.

Think like a mountain climber

Climbing a mountain is one of the most challenging things a person can do. While a successful climb requires physical strength and endurance, resilience and perseverance are even more critical on the journey. Once you begin your climb, you no longer have the option to quit. You must keep going regardless of the adversity you face. Your life depends on it.

However, there is no magic switch that can be flipped the moment you face adversity. Simply telling yourself that you will be resilient and persistent is not enough to develop these traits. Instead, you must adopt the same holistic mental strategy that mountain climbers use to persevere through adversity on their climbs, which includes six parts:

1. Defining your mountain
2. Visualizing
3. Thinking long term
4. Taking it one step at a time
5. Expecting adversity
6. Finishing what you start

By adopting the mindset of a mountain climber, you can learn to focus on the big picture and find the inner strength to persevere through adversity and challenges. This is how you can subconsciously cultivate resilience and perseverance. By consistently reminding yourself of this perspective and striving toward it, you will find yourself becoming more and more capable of facing any obstacle that comes your way.

Define your mountain: If you research the most challenging mountains to climb, you will encounter various suggestions, as the definition of "challenging" varies from person to person. The difficulty of each peak is based on a variety of factors such as altitude, terrain, technicalities (e.g., the use of ropes, harnesses, and specialized gear), and often unpredictable weather patterns.

Despite the variations in opinions, there is a general consensus among lists regarding which peaks are considered the most challenging. The following mountains are commonly recognized as among the most difficult to ascend:

- Mount Everest, also known as the "Roof of the World," is the highest peak in the world, located in the Himalayas between Nepal and Tibet, standing over 29,000 feet tall.
- K2, referred to as the "Savage Mountain," is the second-highest peak in the world, located in Pakistan, and stands over 28,000 feet tall. It is considered to be even more challenging than Mount Everest due to its steep terrain and technical difficulties.
- Nanga Parbat, also known as the "Killer Mountain," while being the ninth-highest peak in the world and standing over 26,500 feet tall, is considered to be one of the most challenging due to its rocky terrain and unpredictable weather conditions.

However, there is always one mountain that is left off any list. That is your personal mental mountain. This is the most challenging climb of them all and a mountain you never stop climbing.

Take it from Jim Whittaker, the first American to summit Mount Everest, who said:

"The biggest mountain you have to climb is the one you build in your mind."

Your mental mountain is composed of two key elements: your goals and your challenges. The goals represent the summit you strive to reach, which is synonymous with the purpose and goals you defined in the previous chapters. The challenges are the obstacles and adversity you must overcome to reach the summit. There will be many different life challenges that make up your unique mountain. Some broad categories include:

- *Emotions* - fears, anxiety, doubts, depression, and lacking self-confidence and self-worth.
- *Relationships* - building and maintaining healthy relationships.
- *Grief and loss* - loss of a loved one, pet, or the end of a relationship.
- *Health and wellness* - managing stress, dealing with sickness, or battling addictions.
- *Career* - job loss, difficulty finding a job, struggling with work-life balance, or feeling unfulfilled.
- *Finances* - difficulties paying bills, debt, managing money, or financial insecurity.
- *Environmental and societal* aspects - dealing with natural disasters or political turmoil.

- *Trauma and abuse* - dealing with emotional, psychological, physical, sexual, or other forms of trauma.
- *Life transitions* - having children, empty nest syndrome, or beginning retirement.

Take a moment to reflect on what challenges make up your current mental mountain. Visualize them in the picture below.

Remember, before people can climb a mountain, they must identify which mountain they are climbing. Just as people have climbed the most challenging mountains in the world, you can climb your mental mountain regardless of how difficult it seems.

Visualization: After climbers determine the mountain they want to climb, the preparation for the climb begins.

Long before setting foot on the mountain, climbers spend time visualizing themselves at the top of the mountain. They develop a clear mental image of what they want to achieve.

Visualization allows climbers to mentally rehearse the climb. They have the opportunity to imagine and plan for a variety of scenarios, obstacles, and adversity they will face.

Visualization is a powerful tool to cultivate resilience and perseverance. It conditions your mind to see success and serves as a motivator on your journey up your mountain, helping you to overcome obstacles and stay focused on your end goal.

There are many examples of successful people who have used visualization to persevere through challenges and achieve success. Athletes use visualization to mentally prepare for competitions, while business leaders and entrepreneurs use it to plan for and achieve growth in their companies. Military personnel, first responders, and healthcare professionals rely on visualization to make quick and effective decisions in high-stress situations. Overall, visualization is a proven technique that can help individuals persevere through challenges and reach their summits. Consider these examples:

- Muhammad Ali, a legendary boxer, used visualization as a key element in his training and preparation for fights. He visualized himself successfully executing moves and ultimately winning. He believed that by visualizing his success, he was conditioning his mind to believe that he could achieve it. This helped him develop the mental and emotional resilience needed to overcome any obstacles he might face in the ring. He once said, *"If my mind can conceive it, and my heart can believe it, then I can achieve it."*

- Jim Carrey, a successful actor, has said, *"I learned many years ago that we become what we imagine."*

- Jack Canfield, author of the best-selling book series *Chicken Soup for the Soul*, claims he visualized himself as a successful author which motivated him to overcome the countless rejection letters he received. He has said, "*The first step in achieving your goal is to take a moment to envision it as if it has already been accomplished.*"

- Lebron James, one of the all-time greatest basketball players, has stated, *"I think visualization is the key to success."*

I even kept a vivid image in my mind of myself holding the first copy of this book, beaming with pride as I posed for a photo with my children. This visualization served as a constant source of motivation, driving me forward even during the most challenging moments when I felt like giving up.

Here is the point: To develop resilience and perseverance, you must visualize yourself on top of your mountain.

Consider the story of Cathy Hughes, founder of Radio One, the largest African American owned and operated broadcast company in the United States. She faced numerous setbacks as a poor black woman on her climb to success. But she displayed an unshakeable belief that "it will work out." She once was asked if this mindset was something she was born with, or if it's something people can learn. She said:

> *"It is definitely an acquired skill. If you allow yourself to be bogged down and lose your enthusiasm, then you are dead in the water. But if you remain optimistic, cheerful, and committed to your goal, there is nothing that can stop you. When you can see it in your mind and believe the day is going to come, you will develop resilience, perseverance, and the grit needed to reach your goal."*

Your takeaway is to begin each day with the end in mind, regardless of where you are. Right now, take a moment to close your eyes and visualize yourself standing at the top of your mountain. Visualize how you will feel in that moment and what you will do to celebrate. *Ingrain that visual in your mind and keep thinking about it during your most challenging times.*

It's this visual that will allow you to build your mental toughness and determination. It will serve as a powerful motivator on your journey up your mountain, helping you persevere through setbacks, obstacles, and difficult times.

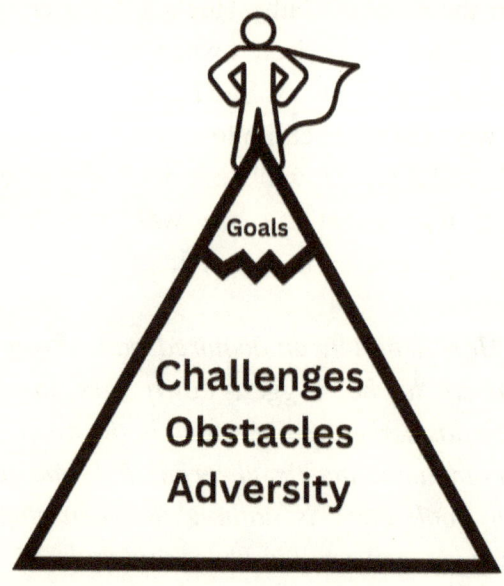

Think long-term: Do you want to know the shortcut to climbing your mountain? There is no shortcut, so stop looking for it.

Climbing a mountain requires time, dedication, and patience to reach the summit. The most experienced climbers know that even though some routes may be considered easier than others, it doesn't mean they will be easy or short. Therefore, climbers pre-commit mentally to the climb being a long-term process.

Studies suggest that mentally pre-committing to something being long-term can lead to the development of resilience and perseverance in the face of short-term setbacks. When you pre-commit to something being long-term, you are essentially telling your mind that setbacks and challenges that occur in the present moment are not the end of the road. This makes it less likely to give up or be discouraged when faced with challenges. It's the motivation you need to stay resilient and persevere.

Take, for example, the journey to becoming a doctor. Most doctors are successful. But becoming a doctor is a long-term journey that is mentally and emotionally challenging, physically demanding, and requires a great deal of dedication, hard work, and perseverance.

A typical path to becoming a doctor includes completing a bachelor's degree, then four years of medical school, followed by several years of residency training. During the years of education, the medical student is exposed to a vast amount of theoretical and practical knowledge, long hours of studying, and intense exams. The entire education and training process can take up to 11-15 years, depending on the specialty!

Becoming a doctor is a challenging and rigorous process that requires a great deal of commitment and sacrifice, to say the least. But most medical students pre-commit to the process being long-term before it even begins. They visualize the impact they will have on people's lives once they become doctors. This long-term perspective, coupled with visualization, helps medical students stay motivated and resilient through years of difficult training.

Success stories don't happen overnight. In reality, the journey to success is often long and filled with failures and challenges. While your mind has been conditioned to think overnight success is the rule, it's the exception. Think about all the stories you hear in the media that only highlight the final outcome but fail to show all the challenges, hard work, and determination over the long term that went into achieving success.

Facebook is a great example of this. While it may appear that Facebook's success was overnight, it was actually the result of several years of hard work, resilience, and perseverance. The early days of the platform were filled with challenges and setbacks. It took years to build the user base and develop the features that made it successful. The illusion of overnight success comes from the fact that the company's growth was exponential, and it reached millions of users in a short period of time. In reality, it took years of hard work and perseverance to get there.

Yes, there may be some illusions that people have reached their summits overnight. Take videos going viral creating instant fame, lottery winners, or businesses hitting big with a product. But these exceptions are just that - exceptions - and they're often short-lived.

In most cases, success stories take years of dedication and perseverance, not just a few days or weeks. It is important to remember that overnight success is often the exception rather than the rule, and that the path to success is usually filled with many obstacles along the way.

As you reach the base of your mental mountain and peer up, remind yourself that the journey is going to be long. Put in the time and have patience. Remain focused on the long term, rather than getting discouraged by short-term setbacks. When you adopt this mindset, you will develop the resilience and perseverance needed to push through short-term setbacks.

The only way to climb a mountain is one step at a time: Mountain climbers know the journey to climb a mountain, no matter how big, requires many small, incremental steps. They remind themselves that progress and success come through consistent and persistent efforts.

They know that each step does not need to take them upward. There will be times when they have to take a step back or move laterally to make progress. In other words, they know the journey to the top is not linear; it's scattered. But it's important to keep moving and not to give up. As Confucius once said:

"It does not matter how slowly you go as long as you do not stop."

Every step is still progress, no matter how small, because small steps add up over time. If you stop taking steps, then you will never reach the summit.

John Wooden, the legendary coach of the UCLA Men's Basketball team, who led his team to ten national titles, holds the record for most consecutive wins (88) and never had a losing season in 27 years as a coach. Wooden is often quoted as saying:

"Little things make big things happen."

Wooden believed in the power of small, daily efforts to achieve greatness, both on and off the court. He believed that it was the accumulation of all these small steps that ultimately led to success.

By taking it one step at a time, you can develop a sense of accomplishment and progress. All too often, we only focus on what we have left to climb and disregard how far we've climbed already. But acknowledging your progress can be a powerful motivator in the face of adversity.

As you stand at the bottom of your mental mountain at an elevation of zero feet, peering up at the daunting peak which seems out of reach, take a deep breath and remind yourself that the only way to climb a mountain is one step at a time.

Don't look at the top of the mountain, look at the step that is in front of you. It's important not to confuse this with the visualization technique. Visualization is about conditioning your mind to see success. You can do this with your eyes closed. However, during the process of your climb, do not look at the distance to the summit. In other words, do not be overwhelmed by the scale of your goals. Instead, focus on the present moment and taking the next step forward. Think about going from zero feet to one foot, then one foot to two feet, then two feet back down to one foot, before you climb higher.

Do not think of going from zero feet to 100 feet in one giant leap. It's not possible. Setting that expectation for yourself will only lead to disappointment and discouragement.

Each day ask yourself: "What is one action I can do today to take my next step?" Remember to count your steps, look down, and see how far you have climbed thus far. Be proud of your wins and progress to date. For example, have you given yourself credit for reading this book up to this point?

In the present moment, your progress may feel and look like the graph shown below:

However, if you zoom your graph out a little, such as a couple of months or years, the progress will feel and look like the graph below:

If you zoom out a little more from the view of your entire life, the progress will feel and look like the graph below:

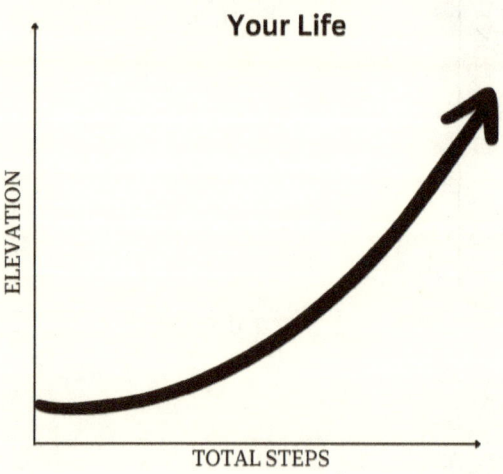

Here is the point: As you gradually zoom out and expand the time frame of your progress assessment, you will notice the journey is actually smoother than it seems in the present moment.

The only way to climb a mountain is one step at a time. Adopting this mindset will help you develop resilience, perseverance, and patience by breaking seemingly insurmountable goals into manageable chunks. When faced with an insurmountable climb, you can be easily discouraged and want to give up the moment you are faced with adversity. But by focusing on the next step in front of you, you'll be motivated to keep going because the step that is in front of you is within reach. The result is that, with time, you will climb higher than you ever could have imagined.

Expect Adversity: Mountain climbers face a wide range of adversities on their climb. Unpredictable weather conditions, treacherous terrain, altitude sickness, risk of injuries, the physiological stress of being on a mountain for extended periods of time, and even self-doubt are some of the challenges that climbers face. It is imperative that climbers have the resilience to persevere through these obstacles to reach their ultimate goal: the summit.

Your mental mountain climb also comes with its own set of adversities. These obstacles may come early in the climb and will likely continue to present themselves as you progress higher. Anticipating these difficulties and committing to facing them head-on will better equip you to navigate them successfully.

While each individual's climb will have its own unique set of adversities, there are certain common challenges that everyone will encounter: the trough of sorrow, self-doubt, and criticism from others. Recognizing that these obstacles are a natural part of the process and pre-committing to pushing through them will help you maintain resilience and persevere on your journey to the summit.

Trough of sorrow: The beginning of a mountain climb is often the easiest. At this stage, climbers are physically and mentally fresh, excited to begin their journeys, and have not yet faced any adversity.

The hardest part of a climb is persevering through the length of the journey after the initial excitement wears off. The climbers encounter their first challenges, and they realize they need to walk laterally for extended distances before they can climb higher.

When you realize that lateral movement without any elevated progress is part of the success process, you will begin to develop resilience and perseverance.

All too often, people commit to an idea, goal, or project but then give up too early. They give up at a point when the initial excitement boost wears off, they encounter their first challenges, and/or everything is taking longer than they hoped.

It's this part of the climb that Paul Graham, best known for his work as a co-founder of the influential startup accelerator, Y Combinator, which has funded revolutionary companies such as Airbnb, Dropbox, Stripe, Instacart, and Reddit, calls the "trough of sorrow." The "trough of sorrow" refers to the time when the initial excitement and optimism subside, challenges become apparent to the team, and progress slows as they begin to feel discouraged and demotivated. It's called the "trough of sorrow" because it's an emotionally trying time for the team. It's adversity. But it's also a normal part of the startup success process. As Paul Graham states:

> *"The trough is the period every startup goes through. It's the period when things are hardest, things are taking longer than you hoped, you are more likely to give up, and where most startups die. But it's also the time when you are closest to success. You just need to persevere through it."*

Companies that understand the "trough of sorrow" as a natural part of the startup journey are more likely to persevere and ultimately find success. On the other hand, those who do not recognize this as a part of the process are more likely to become a statistic among the majority of unsuccessful startups.

Reaching the summit of your mental mountain is similar to the success process of a startup company. Like any new company, your climb starts from the ground up, with no guarantee of success, and the odds of success are not in your favor. However, recognizing the "trough of sorrow" as part of the process makes it more likely that you will persevere to the finish line.

Consider a New Year's resolution, which most people commit to at some point in their lives. The percentage of people who give up on their New Year's resolutions can vary depending on the source and the specific resolution. However, some estimates suggest that a large percentage of people fail to follow through with their New Year's resolutions. According to a study by the University of Scranton, about 80% of New Year's resolutions fail by the second week of February. Another study by Statistic Brain

Research Institute found that only 8% of people achieve their New Year's resolutions.

The month of January can be compared to the initial excitement phase in the "trough of sorrow" graph. But as February approaches, the excitement begins to fade, and the trough of sorrow begins. If people recognized the trough as part of the success process and not the end of the road, they would be more likely to persist rather than give up in the face of adversity.

A common New Year's resolution is to improve one's physical fitness. People often begin with great enthusiasm. But as the weeks pass, the excitement wanes, soreness sets in, and desired physical changes may not be immediately visible. This can lead to a sense of discouragement and the beginning of the trough. By the time February rolls around, many individuals may find themselves back at their starting point from the previous year. In reality, if they had remained committed to their goal and continued to make progress, they may have eventually achieved their fitness goals later in the year.

The point is, to make it more likely that you will reach your summit, recognize the "trough of sorrow" as a natural part of your climb. You will be less inclined to give up and more likely to persist step by step until you reach the summit.

Self-doubt: Even experienced mountain climbers experience self-doubt during the climb. Self-doubt is that little voice inside your head which makes you question your abilities, second-guess your decisions, and lose confidence, and ultimately prevents you from reaching your summit.

However, it's important to remember that self-doubt is just a narrative we create for ourselves, and it's often inaccurate. It's an adversity that touches every individual regardless of his or her level of success or past life experiences. From the entry-level employee to the CEO, from the first-time parent to the seasoned parent, and from the student to the teacher, self-doubt is an inevitable aspect of the human mind.

Even basketball legend Bill Russell, who won 11 NBA championships and was named the league's most valuable player five times, has said:

> *"After my first five games in the league, I started to doubt my abilities."*

The truth is no one has all the answers. We have no way of knowing what lies ahead for us in the future. All we can do is use the information at hand to make the best decision possible and keep moving forward.

Mentally strong and successful people recognize that self-doubt is a normal part of the human mind. They acknowledge it, rather than ignore it, and they don't let it hold them back. Kobe Bryant once said:

> *"Doubt is such a strange thing. You know there will be times when you succeed and there will be times that you fail. So wasting your time, doubting whether you are going to be successful or not, is pointless. It is. You put one foot in front of the other, and then you see what the outcome is. If you*

win, great. You are going to have to wake up the next day and do the journey over again. If you lose, sucks, but you are going to have to wake up the next day and do the journey over again, anyway."

Nevertheless, self-doubt can be incredibly detrimental to a strong mind if left unchecked. It can spread like a disease, clouding your entire perspective with just a drop, much like how a drop of ink can cloud a cup of water.

One drop of self-doubt...   **can cloud your entire mind.**

Consider the fear many people have with public speaking. According to the National Institute of Mental Health, 74% of people experience some form of public speaking anxiety. Self-doubt is a major contributor to this fear.

The self-doubt individuals may experience when it comes to public speaking can have a cascading effect on their mental and emotional states. It starts with a seed of doubt in their abilities to effectively deliver a speech or present information, which can quickly grow into fears of failure, increased anxiety, and physical symptoms such as sweating, shaking, and rapid heartbeat. This initial self-doubt can spiral into a cycle of negative thoughts and more self-doubt, making it more likely for people to experience the worst-case scenario of their minds going blank during the speech. The fear of not being able to think on their feet and improvise if needed can further fuel their anxiety, making it even harder to overcome their self-doubt and perform well in a public setting.

It's essential to be prepared for self-doubt, recognize it, and remember that it's simply a narrative that your mind has created. It's just a thought, not a reality. Don't let it cloud your confidence, hold you back, or prevent you from moving forward. Be mindful of self-doubt and you will be able to overcome it.

Believing in oneself and having a positive outlook on the future is crucial for overcoming self-doubt. This mindset is shared by the most mentally strong and successful individuals, regardless of their professions or backgrounds. This applies to everyone, including students, teachers, parents, athletes, or businesspersons. For example:

- Theodore Roosevelt, the 26th President of the United States and Noble Peace Prize winner, once said, *"Believe you can and you're halfway there."*
- Wayne Gretzky, considered one of the greatest hockey players of all time, has said, *"Having belief in yourself is ¾ of the battle."*

- Eric Thomas, a successful motivational speaker, author, and minister, has said about success, *"You have to see it when nobody else sees it, feel it when it's not tangible, and believe it when you cannot see it."*

- Howard Schultz, the CEO of Starbucks who helped grow the brand from a small local business to thousands of locations all over the world, has said, *"There is a tendency when you have had some success for people to assume you have all the answers. And I didn't have all the answers back then and I don't have all the answers now. In 1987, Starbucks had 11 stores, but we had a dream to build a national brand. We had no experience building a national brand, but we had a passion and most importantly, the BELIEF that we could build it."*

Ultimately, resilience is about reminding yourself that you're human. Self-doubt is something everyone deals with, even if you can't see it.

Have you heard of *imposter syndrome*? It's the psychological phenomenon in which you doubt your capabilities, hear that little voice inside your head whispering "You are a fraud," and have a fear of being exposed as an imposter despite previous evidence of your competence.

Remember, you are stronger than you think. Many people often forget that you're allowed to make mistakes, take a few steps back, and walk laterally. You can't have success without making mistakes and taking risks. But if you believe you can do it, then at some point, you will persevere through the adversity of self-doubt.

Criticism: Climbers know that the rain and snow will come as they climb higher and higher up the mountain. They cannot control the weather, but they can control their reaction to it. They do not let the rain and snow deter them from their goal: the summit. They may adjust their path, seeking shelter or finding an alternative route, but they do not deviate from their ultimate goal to reach the top. A successful climber embraces the challenge, knowing that it is through persevering through rain and snow that the summit can be reached.

Criticism can be thought of as unpredictable rain or snow on a mountain climb. Think of each raindrop or snowflake as a different person's opinion or judgment of your actions. Criticism can be unexpected, unrelenting, and overwhelming at times, causing you to question your decisions and reconsider the route you are climbing.

But just as climbers don't let the rain and snow deter them from reaching the summit, you should not let criticism discourage you from reaching your goals. People who stop climbing the moment they face criticism will miss out on the potential success of their endeavors.

It is important to acknowledge that any endeavor that challenges the status quo is bound to face resistance. History is full of examples of innovations that, despite initial resistance, went on to improve the world in remarkable ways. The leaders behind these innovations did not let criticism deter them from their summits.

Consider the following world-changing inventions. You would laugh to even think that these were resisted and met with criticism at one point:

- **Cars** - The Model T came out in 1908 but faced resistance from certain cities who drafted laws to outlaw it. If the leaders behind the car industry had given up at the first sign of resistance, we would still be using the horse and buggy as our primary mode of transportation today!
- **Planes** - The Wright brothers faced skepticism and mockery with their prototype in 1903, but they persevered and improved their design. Today, airplanes are a vital part of modern transportation, connecting people and cultures around the world.
- **The iPhone** - First released in 2007, it faced criticism for being overpriced and lacking in features. But it revolutionized the way we communicate and access information. It has become one of the most popular and influential devices of all time.

Or consider the following mentally strong and successful people who did not let criticism deter them from reaching their goals:

- Martin Luther King Jr. faced intense criticism and resistance while he strived for equality for African Americans. His perseverance and determination led to the

Civil Rights Act of 1964 and the Voting Rights Act of 1965, which had a profound impact on American society.

- Mahatma Gandhi faced intense resistance as he advocated for India's independence.

- Nelson Mandela spent 27 years in prison as he advocated ending apartheid and establishing a democratic government in South Africa.

- Malala Yousafzai faced extreme resistance for her activism for girls' education in Pakistan. She even survived an assassination attempt by the Taliban. However, she continued her advocacy on the importance of girls' education globally and became the youngest Nobel Prize winner.

- Albert Einstein faced rejection and criticism from the scientific community, but persevered and eventually developed the theory of general relativity, which revolutionized our understanding of the universe.

Imagine what the world would be like today if these individuals gave up at the first sign of criticism.

Even I know that despite my best efforts to create a clear and actionable book that is easy for readers to understand, there will always be some who critique it as being written at a lower level or as a compilation of common knowledge. They may say that the techniques outlined in this book are not new or they can't be implemented. Some may find the book too long, while others may find it too short. Some may say it is overly simplistic, while others may say it's too complicated. There is always going to be something, but I will not let these criticisms discourage me from continuing to help people build mental strength to live better lives.

It's important to remember that criticism is a part of life. It will rain down on you. You cannot avoid it because people have different tastes, and it is impossible to please everyone. Take a look at any online review of the best books, movies, art, products, or services. None are perfect. They all receive bad reviews.

What's important is to learn how to handle criticism so you can use it to improve, rather than let it discourage you.

Developing resilience and perseverance can be accomplished by separating your self-worth from criticism. When you don't take things personally, you'll be able to maintain a positive self-image despite receiving negative feedback.

The two types of criticism: It's important to distinguish between the two types of criticism you will receive and to approach each one with a different mindset. Criticism will either be constructive or destructive.

Constructive criticism is intended to help you improve and grow. It is specific, objective, and offered in a way that you can understand and apply it. *Be open to constructive criticism. Use it as a learning opportunity to grow.*

On the other hand, destructive criticism is intended to hurt or demean you. It is often vague, subjective, and delivered in a way that is hurtful and unhelpful. This includes personal attacks, name-calling, and negative judgment.

A majority of the criticism you receive will be destructive. To help navigate this, consider the Pareto Principle, also known as the 80/20 rule. This principle states that 80% of effects come from 20% of causes. In other words, a small number of inputs are responsible for a majority of the results. Applying this to navigating criticism, roughly 20% of the criticism you receive is constructive and can be used for personal growth. The remaining 80% is probably not helpful and should likely be ignored. Keep this balance in mind to help you filter out destructive criticism.

Ultimately, mentally strong and successful people don't allow others' opinions to define them, and they don't let criticism stop them from pursuing their climbs. As you encounter criticism on your climb, don't let that discourage you, shift your focus, or cast self-doubt. This is how you develop resilience and perseverance to overcome adversity.

Finish what you start: What do you think would happen to mountain climbers if they started their climb and then quit in the middle? When they are on the mountain, they have no choice but to be resilient, persevere, and finish the climb.

To develop resilience and perseverance, you must always commit to finishing what you start. A true measure of success is in the ability to finish what you have started. There's a common phrase that successful people say:

> *"How you do anything is how you do everything."*

Whether it is a small task such as washing dishes or a larger undertaking like writing a book, every time you finish something, you develop and improve your mental habit of resilience and perseverance because you are conditioning your mind to do whatever it takes to complete that task or goal.

Conversely, every time you choose not to finish, you develop a mental habit of giving up in the face of adversity. What do you expect will happen the next time you face adversity, if you previously conditioned your mind to stop when something gets difficult?

A person with a weak mindset will give up easily and attribute others' success to factors such as talent or luck. However, true success is often the result of persistence and determination to see something through to completion.

This is what all mentally strong and successful people have in common. They just don't give up. They don't stop in the middle when things become difficult. They stop when they get to the end.

They recognize seeing something through to the end is not just about achieving the original goal. It's about developing resilience and perseverance that can help them with future endeavors. They recognize that change happens in the moment you want to quit, but don't.

Consider the story of George Lucas, an American filmmaker best known for creating the Star Wars and Indiana Jones franchises. Despite facing numerous obstacles and setbacks, he never gave up on his dream of making films. He has said:

> *"I never left anything unfinished. I might not have finished it as well as I wanted, but I finished it."*

Ultimately, his determination to see things through to the end eventually led him to achieve great success in creating the Star Wars and Indiana Jones franchises, some of the highest-grossing film series of all time.

The takeaway is to be less concerned with the actual outcome and more concerned with the mental habit you are building. Seeing something through to the end develops resilience and perseverance. It develops a strong mind to overcome future challenges.

Imagine you begin painting a wall in your home but give up halfway through because it becomes too difficult. Not only will the wall remain unfinished, but you will also feel disappointed and discouraged every time you look at the wall. On the other hand, if you push through and finish the wall, not only will the wall be completed, but you will also have gained a sense of resilience and perseverance knowing you can complete a task.

There is one more key point to remember: It's important to know when to let things go and move on. For example, if you don't like the color of the wall after it is finished, choose a new color and repaint it. If you achieve a weight loss goal but find that it is not making you feel better, reevaluate and adjust your target weight to a number that is more suitable for you. If you finish writing a book but realize that being an author is not for you, let go of that pursuit and find something that aligns better with your interests and goals.

When you finish tasks, you build resilience and perseverance that can be carried forward to other areas of life. But you don't need to carry the actual outcome with you for the rest of your life. Let things go when you feel it's appropriate but always take with you the resilience and perseverance you developed by seeing the journey through to the end. In the end, you will be more equipped to conquer your next mountain.

With that, I'll leave you with one of the most prolific examples of resilience and perseverance. Thomas Edison, when asked how it feels to fail 1,000 times, responded:

"I have found 1,000 ways not to make a light bulb, but I will find the way that will work."

—*Thomas Edison*

And in 1879, after years of trying, he did just that.

TRAIT 5

CREATE YOUR OWN LUCK

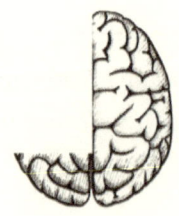

Have you ever looked at someone else and thought, "Wow, they are so lucky"? Have you ever felt envious of those around you who seem to have all the luck in the world? Have you ever considered your own fortune to be less than others? The good news is you are not alone. Most people have felt this way at some point in their lives.

Many people believe that success is dependent on luck and that luck is based on destiny. They assume certain individuals are simply born with good luck and that their success is predetermined. When we see someone who is successful, accomplished, or wealthy, we might say, *"They were just in the right place at the right time," "They had everything handed to them,"* or *"They were born with a silver spoon in their mouth."*

This is the mindset of a weak person and is prevalent in all aspects of life, including personal life, career, education, and sports. It's a mindset that is limiting and demotivating, as it implies that we have no control over our own success. Weak-minded people think that luck and success are the results of destiny without considering all the effort, work, and mental strength that went into achieving it.

But what if I told you that you have the power to create your own luck, that you are not at the mercy of destiny, and that you have the power to shape your life with the right mindset, choices, and actions? Successful people understand that they are not merely at the mercy of fate:

- Thomas Jefferson, the third President of the United States and author of the Declaration of Independence, said, *"The harder I work, the more luck I seem to have."*
- Gary Player, considered one of the greatest golfers of all time, said, *"The more I practice, the luckier I get."*
- Douglas Macarthur, an American five-star general, said, *"The best luck of all is the luck you create for yourself."*
- J. Paul Getty, the founder of the Getty Oil Company and one of the richest men in the world during his lifetime, said, *"You can't rely on luck. You have to create it."*
- Gary Vaynerchuk, a serial entrepreneur, and bestselling author, said, *"The more you hustle, the more luck you have."*
- Ray Kroc, who turned McDonald's into one of the most successful fast-food corporations in

the world, said, *"Luck is a dividend of sweat. The more you sweat, the luckier you get."*

- Brian Chesky, a co-founder of Airbnb, said, *"Recognize luck is a huge part of success, but you can create your own luck."*

Or consider all comments from every successful person interviewed on "How I Built This," which is a podcast that tells the stories of entrepreneurs, innovators, and idealists, and the movements they built. Each episode focuses on the journey of a particular business or person from the humble beginnings to eventual success. Host Guy Raz speaks with the founders and key players behind some of the world's best-known companies and brands, delving into the inspiration, setbacks, and lessons learned along the way. The show provides a glimpse into the creative process, perseverance, and hard work that goes into building a successful business.

At the end of each interview, Guy Raz asks the guests about the role of luck in their success. He asks: *"How much of your success do you think was based on luck, and how much was based on hard work?"*

The majority of the interviewees responded with some variation of the same answer. They acknowledge that luck played a part in their success, but they also emphasize that their efforts put them in the right place at the right time to create their own luck. For example, consider the responses from some of the most successful founders:

- Kevin Systrom, a co-founder of Instagram, said, *"Actually, I have this thesis that the world runs on luck. The question is what you do with it. Everyone gets lucky for some amount of their life and the question is are you alert enough to know you are being lucky or becoming lucky? Are you talented enough to take that advantage and run with it, and do you have enough grit and resilience to stay with it when it gets hard? Because everyone gets lucky in minimal ways every week. You find a dollar on the ground, get a break at work to work on a cool project, or you meet someone really interesting. The difference between people who succeed in the long run and the people who don't is frankly that optimism that you got lucky and now it's yours to make awesome. The question is can you take that luck and capitalize on it?"*

- Barbara Corcoran, a real estate mogul and widely known as an investor on the TV show *Shark Tank*, said, *"I do believe in luck. I had many lucky breaks. But I realized, once you grow up, you make your own luck. You definitely make your own luck. I think all the lucky breaks I had were more a result of me <u>staying in the game</u>, just believing something would break, and hanging around long* *enough. That's more important than actual luck."*

- Melanie Perkins, the founder of Canva, said, *"It's an interesting question. I think that if you zoom out of luck and think about where you were born, who were your parents, what was your education, and having good health, I couldn't be luckier. But then on the other side of it, I feel like we <u>planted enough seeds</u> that eventually one of those grew. So that's another version of luck. We planted 1,000 seeds and one of those grew. So, the luck came from the hard work of planting 1,000 seeds."*

- Joel Clark, the founder of Kodiak Cakes, said, *"People always say that fish don't just jump in your boat. But I say you still got to be out fishing to catch fish."*

So, how can you create your own luck? The trick to building mental strength is to think of creating your own luck like a math formula. Each step, like an input in the calculation, builds on the previous one. Skipping any step in the math formula will result in an incorrect outcome. In other words, if you don't take the necessary actions and make calculated decisions, you will not be able to create your own luck. But, when all the steps are followed correctly with time and effort, the final outcome will equal the luck you've created, leading to success.

The "create your own luck" formula consists of the following variables:

+   Recognizing that success is not a percentage game
+   Taking calculated risks
+   Preparing
+   Socializing
-     Removing your emotions
+   Developing resilience and perseverance
=   Luck

Success is not a percentage game

Successful people understand that taking risks is an inherent part of creating your own luck on the journey to success. Those who have accomplished great things have done so by stepping out of their comfort zones and embracing the uncertainty that comes with taking a risk.

For example, Jeff Bezos took a risk by quitting his high-paying corporate job to start an online bookstore. Sara Blakely took a risk by investing $5,000, which was her life savings at the time, to create Spanx. Melanie Perkins took a risk by pursuing a new business model in the graphic design industry.

However, too often people are afraid to take risks because the probability of failure is often high and the success rate is low. The low success rate often holds people back from pursuing new opportunities that could lead to success.

But these people are thinking about it all wrong and playing on the wrong field. Success is not measured by the percentage of times you are successful. Instead, it's measured on the magnitude of what is accomplished.

People don't care how many times you fail or how low your success rate is. It doesn't matter if you fail a million times and your success rate is less than 1%. As Mark Cuban, billionaire and owner of the Dallas Mavericks, said:

"You only have to be right once. People don't remember all my failures, all the companies that came and went. But you're right one time and now all of a sudden people call you an overnight success story, even though it might have been ten years in the making...If you keep on grinding, keep learning, keep going forward, all it takes is just one."

In other words, all it takes is one accomplishment to be successful. To put this in perspective, Geno Auriemma is considered to be one of the greatest women's college basketball coaches of all time. He's best known for winning 11 national championships. But did you know he lost ten times in the Final Four? That means he lost almost half as many times as he won when his team reached the Final Four. Yet he is still viewed as extremely successful. Or consider Michael Jordan, who missed over 50% of the shots he took in his career, yet he's still considered to be one of the best basketball players of all time.

The first variable in creating your own luck is recognizing that success is not a percentage game. Otherwise, you'll be playing the game of life on the wrong field. Think of it like playing a sport. You can't win a basketball game on a soccer field, just as you can't be successful in life if you are mentally playing on the wrong field. Take a step off of the percentages field, and take a step onto the numbers field.

Creating your own luck is about recognizing that all it takes is one opportunity to succeed. When you think and work from this perspective, you will be more likely to take calculated risks, which is the next variable in the formula to create your own luck.

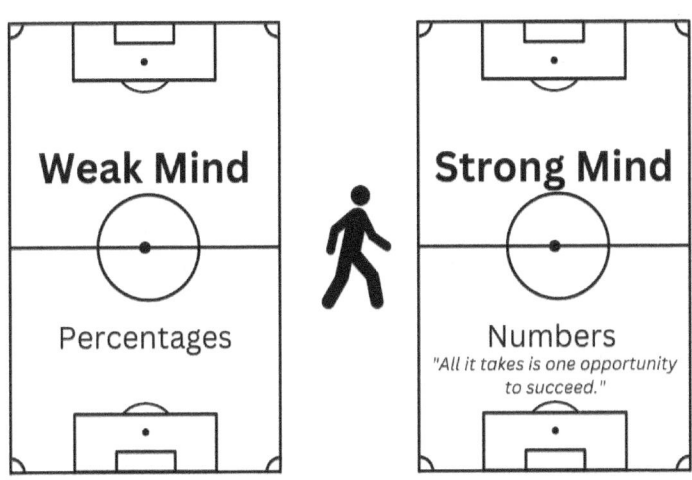

Take calculated risks

Creating your own luck is about trying a lot of things and planting a lot of seeds. Now that you are no longer concerned with your rate of success, you are mentally ready to plant thousands of seeds by taking calculated risks. Mark Cuban often credits his success to this strategy, by trying a lot of things from a young age, including selling baseball cards, candies, and stamps, as well as founding and selling MicroSolutions, a computer company, and broadcast.com, an internet radio company that he sold for $5.7 billion to Yahoo!.

It's important to understand that calculated risks are different from other types of risks. Calculated risks are based on analysis and thoughtful consideration. It's not just about doing thousands of random things, which is bound to yield limited results. For example, Cuban recognized he was good at sales, so he focused his efforts on selling.

Imagine a farmer planting thousands of seeds, with the knowledge that not all will flourish. The difference between a successful harvest and a mediocre one lies in the approach. Farmers who meticulously plan their planting, considering the right location, timing, soil, and care, will undoubtedly reap a richer harvest compared to ones who randomly scatter their seeds without thought. In other words, one farmer is taking calculated risks, and the other is taking uncalculated risks.

The technique for calculating a risk lies in your thought process. To do it effectively, you need to anticipate opportunities, understand odds and probabilities, do the high-level aggregate math, objectively consider the "range" of possible outcomes for each individual risk, and overcome analysis paralysis. Neglecting these steps is essentially gambling, and you'll likely experience negative outcomes in the long run.

Anticipate: Anticipation is a crucial factor in taking calculated risks. Successful people take calculated risks to put themselves in a position for success to come to them, instead of chasing success. Wayne Gretzky's success is a prime example of the power of anticipation. He famously said:

*"Skate to where the puck is going, not where it
is."*

This reflects his exceptional ability to anticipate the movement of the puck and position himself accordingly. This allowed him to stay ahead of the competition, see and create opportunities, and make effective moves on the ice.

By constantly anticipating the location of the puck, Gretzky put himself in a position where success came to him. This made him one of the greatest scorers of all time. If he had been skating only to where the puck was, he would have constantly been chasing success.

When calculating risk, ask yourself: *"Am I positioning myself for success to come to me, or am I chasing it?"* If it's the latter, it's an uncalculated risk. If it's the former, it's a calculated risk.

Rosalind Brewer, the CEO of Walgreens and former CEO of Sam's Club and Group President of Starbucks, is renowned for her exceptional sense of anticipation. She encourages others to think ahead and be proactive in their approach to success by saying:

*"Think about what's next, after what's next, and
look around the corner of the corner."*

This mindset has helped her achieve significant success throughout her career, as she positioned herself to take advantage of new opportunities and stay ahead of the competition.

Here's the point: The key to successful calculated risk-taking lies in anticipating future opportunities, rather than merely reacting to the present. By planting your seeds where future opportunities are likely to arise, you position yourself to capitalize on them as they come, rather than constantly chasing after success. It's important to think ahead and focus on where opportunities are going, not just where they are currently visible. Those who take risks based solely on the current landscape will always struggle, as they'll constantly be pursuing success instead of having it come to them.

Understand odds and probabilities: The game of poker is played with a standard deck of 52 cards. The objective is to win each pot by having the best five-card hand. While players have a few chances to switch some of their cards for new ones, the players eventually have to play the hands they are dealt. Because of this, some people say poker is a game of luck, where the cards that are dealt determine the winner.

However, the most successful players know that winning the overall game depends on much more than just the five cards in each hand. Winning the overall game is actually the result of executing well-thought-out strategies, understanding odds and probabilities, and taking calculated risks based on those odds and probabilities.

Consider this statement from Phil Hellmuth, 14-time World Series of Poker bracelet winner, who has said:

THE POSIMISTIQ MIND

"Poker is not just about luck. Luck is a factor, but strategy is a much more important factor in determining who wins and loses. You can create your own luck."

Ultimately, success comes down to betting more chips when you have stronger hands and betting fewer chips, or even folding, when you have weaker hands.

In poker, hand strength is determined by rarity and the odds of obtaining certain card combinations. A High Card, being the most common and least valuable hand, has odds of 1 in 1. A One Pair, consisting of two cards of the same rank, has odds of 1 in 2 and is slightly more powerful. A Three of a Kind consisting of three cards of the same rank has odds of 1 in 47, making it even more powerful. A Four of a Kind has odds of 1 in 4,165, which is even more powerful. The ultimate hand to have in poker is the Royal Flush, consisting of Ace, King, Queen, Jack, and Ten of the same suit. With odds of approximately 1 in 649,740, it is a rare and unbeatable combination, making it the most powerful hand in the game. When a player holds a Royal Flush, they "go all in."

In life, you have the power to create favorable outcomes over the long term by utilizing a strategic approach similar to that in the game of poker. Poker players may be able to bluff their way through a weak hand and win the occasional pot by making other players fold. But leveraging *only* their weak hands in the long term will eventually lead to failure.

You need to identify your strong hands and bet more chips accordingly. It's a calculated risk worth taking.

The way you play your strong hands is to identify your five greatest strengths and use them simultaneously to your advantage.

For example, playing with one strength, like having a High Card, may lead to some victories, but it is unlikely to be a consistent winning strategy because it is the most common. However, pairing two strengths, which is like pairing two cards of the same rank, increases your chances of winning. Combining three strengths together, like combining three cards of the same rank, further increases your chances of success, and so on.

The ultimate hand to play in poker is the Royal Flush. Combining your five greatest strengths together is like betting on the Royal Flush. The odds are very low that anyone can compete with you, thus increasing your chances of success. Your Royal Flush is what makes you unique.

Let's put this into perspective. One of your greatest strengths might be math. There are plenty of people who are also great at math, so it will be tough to create a competitive advantage over those people. But another one of your strengths might be storytelling. There are certainly fewer people whose strengths are math *and* storytelling. With less competition, your odds of success in a field that requires both math and storytelling increase. Imagine how your odds of winning will continue to increase as you add in your three other strengths and complete your Royal Flush.

Combining multiple strengths together is how you create your own luck and how people become successful. The goal is to find something where you can use as many of your strengths as possible.

Think about Gary Kasparov, the renowned chess grandmaster known for his strategic thinking, tactical abilities, and passion for the game of chess. If he had focused on cooking, he probably wouldn't have reached the same level of success because he wouldn't have been utilizing and leveraging his three greatest strengths. Jake Shimabukuro, the acclaimed ukulele musician known for his musical creativity and stage presence, probably wouldn't have achieved the same level of recognition if he focused on art, instead of playing a musical instrument.

Or consider an insurance company searching for a new CEO. The company must choose between two candidates, both with prior CEO experience. However, one candidate has an added background in the insurance industry, while the other has experience in the consumer products industry. It's likely that the company will choose the candidate with experience in the insurance industry as it is another strength that maximizes the candidate's (and therefore the company's) chances of success.

My own "Royal Flush" consists of my ability and passion to motivate people, having resilience and perseverance, storytelling, practicing mental strength, and the ability to make complex topics easy to understand.

As I thought about how I could play these strengths to the fullest, I envisioned many things. For example, I could have written an article on mental strength, but writing an article takes much less work than writing a book, so I wouldn't have been utilizing my strength of resilience and perseverance. If I tried to write a book on quantum physics, to help others understand it, it wouldn't be as successful as writing a book about mental strength, something I know a lot about and am passionate about.

To be clear, you can't always avoid weak hands. Sometimes you have to play them too. It's important to acknowledge and work on areas of improvement so your weak hands don't hold you back. But you must also recognize that you can't go all-in every day with your weak hands and expect to succeed. The long-term odds just aren't in your favor.

So, identify your top five strengths and try to combine as many of them together as you can. The more you can combine your strengths and identify an area where they can be utilized together, the greater your chances of success. And if you are able to find an area where you can play your Royal Flush, that is when you can have the most success. Bet on your Royal Flush as much as possible. The odds are heavily in your favor. It is a calculated risk worth taking.

Do the high-level *aggregate* math: Jeff Bezos once said:

> *"Given a 10% chance of a 100 times payoff, you should take that bet every time. But you're still going to be wrong nine times out of ten. We all know that if you swing for the fences, you're going to strike out a lot, but you're also going to hit some home runs."*

The math here is clear. Based on the law of large numbers, the overall outcome will be positive. If you take ten risks that you'll either lose $10 or win 100 times that amount, you will make a profit of $1,000 from the one successful outcome and incur a loss of $90 from the nine failed attempts. Despite the majority of outcomes being unsuccessful, the aggregate impact of all ten occurrences will be a positive gain of $910.

- *Success return = risk * return * number of occurrences out of ten*
  - *$10*100*1 = $1,000*
- *Failure return = risk * return * number of occurrences out of ten*
  - *$10*-1*9 = -$90*

I recognize that real-life decision-making may not be as straightforward, and numerical calculations may not always be applicable. Sometimes the benefits may be qualitative, such as increased satisfaction or improved relationships. However, it's essential to consider the estimated probabilities and returns, both quantitative and qualitative, of potential outcomes in order to make informed calculated risks.

For example, imagine yourself as a lawyer seeking to expand your professional network. You're presented with ten upcoming networking events. Although there is no guarantee of success at each event, you recognize that making even one strong connection could lead to acquiring a new client, who becomes a loyal and reliable source of business over time. That connection not only brings you consistent income (quantitative payoff) but also the opportunity to build and reinforce your reputation (qualitative payoff). That quantitative and qualitative return of making a connection should be enough for you to take the calculated risk of attending all ten networking events.

The point is, when the overall calculation shows a strong likelihood of a positive outcome, then it's a calculated risk worth taking. You should plant a seed there.

Remember, the key to creating your own luck is taking *multiple* calculated risks, not just one. Over time, the odds will work in your favor, even though not every calculated risk will lead to the desired outcome.

Objectively consider the range of possible outcomes for each *individual* risk: Let's face it, taking risks always involves an element of uncertainty. No matter how much you anticipate, calculate, plan, and prepare, the future is unpredictable, and there is no guarantee of a specific outcome.

Given the inherent uncertainty in taking risks, it's crucial to consider the range of possible outcomes before taking each risk.

The key word here is "range." Rather than trying to predict a specific outcome, which is often impossible, the focus should be on creating a range of outcomes that the actual outcome is most likely to fall within. This approach allows for more informed decision-making and helps you feel more confident and prepared, regardless of the actual outcome. If you are comfortable with the range of possible outcomes, it's a sign that the risk is calculated and worth taking.

A common pitfall in considering the range of possible outcomes is a disproportionate focus on pessimism and overemphasis on the worst-case scenario. This narrow perspective ignores the potential positive outcomes or undervalues their significance. This kind of thinking can lead to the inability to take calculated risks.

It's important to keep a balanced view and weigh the range of possible outcomes objectively to make informed decisions and approach each risk with confidence.

Here's the technique to maintain a balanced perspective when considering the range of possible outcomes: For every downside scenario you imagine, envision an equal and realistic upside scenario. For instance, if you're worried about losing $50,000, imagine making $50,000 as well (if it's realistic). If your worst-case scenario is losing your job, then the corresponding positive scenario is getting a better job opportunity. If your worst-case scenario is wasting time on a project, then the corresponding positive scenario is learning valuable lessons for future endeavors.

To identify a full range of possible outcomes of an individual risk, write down three different scenarios for both the positive and negative outcomes, each with an increasing level of magnitude. This magnitude could be categorized as low, medium, and high (or minimal, moderate, and maximum). For example, consider the range of possible outcomes for a high school student considering college:

Magnitude	Realistic Negative Outcomes	Realistic Positive Outcomes
Minimal	Struggle to form meaningful connections.	Make lifelong friends.
Moderate	Gain knowledge and skills that are not directly relevant to their ultimate career path.	Gain a wealth of knowledge and skills.
Maximum	Accumulate student debt that delays or impedes financial independence.	Secure a lucrative and fulfilling job.

Or consider the range of possible outcomes for a person considering a new job:

Magnitude	Realistic Negative Outcomes	Realistic Positive Outcomes
Minimal	Struggle to fit in with coworkers.	Make lifelong friends and connections.

| Moderate | Face challenging work responsibilities and increased stress levels. | Learn new skills, grow professionally, and have optimal work-life balance. |
| Maximum | Get laid off due to restructuring. | Get promoted to the highest role. |

After you have identified the full range of realistic outcomes, and if you can confidently say that you are prepared and willing to accept any outcome within the established range, then the risk you are considering is a calculated one worth taking.

Overcome analysis paralysis: Having calculated the high-level math and visualized the range of possible outcomes, it's time to take the calculated risk. But many find that the presence of uncertainty and the abundance of options often leads to analysis paralysis.

Analysis paralysis is a relatively common phenomenon among people of all ages and backgrounds. It occurs in all aspects of life where a decision needs to be made, whether it's personal or professional. The greater the decision, the greater the paralysis. The overwhelming amount of information available to us and the fear of making the wrong decision can often lead to a state of analysis paralysis, making it difficult to act, which leads to missed opportunities. Can you think of a time you have experienced this phenomenon?

One common example is breaking up with a significant other. This can be a challenging and emotional experience. For many, the indecision and overthinking that comes with it can become even more difficult to handle. Analysis paralysis sets in as people spend an excessive amount of time weighing the pros and cons, predicting the future, and considering all possible outcomes, leading to a cycle of indecision and missed opportunities. In the end, prolonging the decision-making process only extends the period of unhappiness for both partners and can result in missed opportunities for growth and moving forward.

Here's the point: Don't let the fear of the unknown hold you back from taking the risk you calculated.

To overcome this challenge, first establish a firm deadline for making a decision. This will give you a clear timeline for action and help you avoid prolonged indecision. While we discussed how deadlines are often arbitrary and flexible in the chapter, "Silence the Noise," setting a deadline can also be a helpful tool in motivating yourself to reach your goals.

Next, boost your confidence by trusting the efficiency of the calculation process. Keep in mind that the calculation process is built on the principle of the law of large numbers, meaning it is meant to deliver consistent results over time, but not necessarily with each specific calculated risk you take. By acknowledging that not every calculated risk may bring favorable results, you've already prepared yourself to handle setbacks, which can reduce feelings of stress, anxiety, and indecision.

Finally, take some comfort knowing that even the unsuccessful risks still provide valuable learning experiences, knowledge, and insights that can be applied to your future endeavors.

Think about all the times you have heard someone express regret for missed opportunities. They say things like, *"I wish I had invested in that piece of real estate,"* *"I wish I had taken that job offer,"* or *"I wish I had done _____."* However, rarely do you ever hear people say, *"I wish I never took that chance."*

Embrace the opportunity to create your own luck and success by taking calculated risks. Remember, if you have taken the time to anticipate, do the math, and carefully consider the range of possible outcomes, then you have executed the process of calculating a risk. Don't let indecision hold you back from success. Imagine looking back on your life from the end and ask yourself what you want to see. Do you want to look back with regret for missed opportunities and indecision, or do you want to look back having satisfaction in the calculated risks you took and the chances you embraced, regardless of the actual outcomes?

Before moving on to the next section, consider the following real-life examples to better understand the distinction between calculated and uncalculated risks.

Situation	Uncalculated Risk	Calculated Risk
Entrepreneurs starting a business or launching a new product	Invest in something without researching market, competitors, costs, and potential for success.	Conduct market research, create a detailed business plan, and assess the potential risks and rewards associated with the venture.
Young professionals considering a career change	Quit their current jobs to figure out their lives.	Consider the potential benefits such as greater job satisfaction and higher pay, against the potential negatives such as the need for additional education or training, lower pay during the transition, and uncertainty about future job stability.
Doctors performing surgery	Ignore a patient's medical history, which could lead to adverse reactions or worsened medical condition.	Assess the patient's medical history, evaluate the risks and benefits of the procedure, and consider alternative treatment options.
Lawyers taking on a challenging case	Represent a client without considering their own experience and potential damage	Assess the strengths and weaknesses of the case, evaluate the potential

	to their reputation in the event of a lost case.	outcomes, and consider the impact of the case on their reputation.
Making investments	Invest in a single stock without properly researching the company.	Diversify a portfolio that is aligned with the investor's financial goals and considers current market conditions.
High school students considering college	Follow their friends by choosing the same school or major, without considering the long-term impacts such as lower earning potential and limited job prospects, or attend an expensive school without considering the high student debt they will incur.	Research colleges and programs, assess the potential outcomes such as increased earning potential and job opportunities, and consider the costs and benefits of attending before investing time and money into obtaining a higher education.

Preparation

If you are given the choice to select between winning and losing, what would you choose? Most people would choose to win.

But even though most people want to win, not everybody wants to *prepare* to win. Preparation is what sets mentally strong and successful people apart from mentally weak and unsuccessful people.

Mike Krzyzewski, Hall of Fame basketball coach who led Duke University Men's Basketball team to five national championships and the United States Men's Basketball team to the gold medal in the 2008 Olympics, has said:

> *"Winners expect to win, all people want to win, but the real winners know how to prepare to win. At times you are going to have to learn to do things you don't like to do or are not good at. But if you can learn to like the things you don't like to do, then you become somebody who loves the process more than the execution. You become Kobe Bryant, and he was the most prepared player I've ever been around."*

Creating your own luck through effective preparation can be achieved by following two fundamental principles:

1. Preparation * timing = luck
2. Don't practice until you get it right. Practice until you can't get it wrong.

Preparation * timing = luck: Mentally strong and successful people recognize that luck is the eventual intersection of preparation and timing. When exactly they will intersect is uncertain. What is certain is that a lack of preparation eliminates any chance of reaching the intersection of luck. Think of this like a math formula. Without either variable, luck cannot be created.

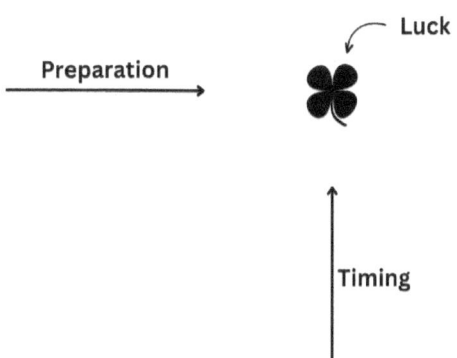

There is a common mantra among many athletes, military personnel, motivational speakers, and other successful people:

"If you stay ready, you will never need to get ready."

To be clear, it's not about having a rigid structure or living in a constant state of paranoia. It's about preparing every day to achieve success. This can include activities such as researching things within your industry to stay up to date on the latest developments in your field, learning new skills, networking, practicing, or taking calculated risks.

The reality is that opportunities can arise unexpectedly, and it's crucial to be prepared to seize them when they do. You never know when an opportunity will arise to advance your career, make a valuable connection, or learn a new skill. By consistently engaging in preparatory actions, you increase your chances of success and create opportunities for the right timing (and therefore luck) to cross your path. But if you have to take time to get ready when an opportunity presents itself, you may miss the opportunity.

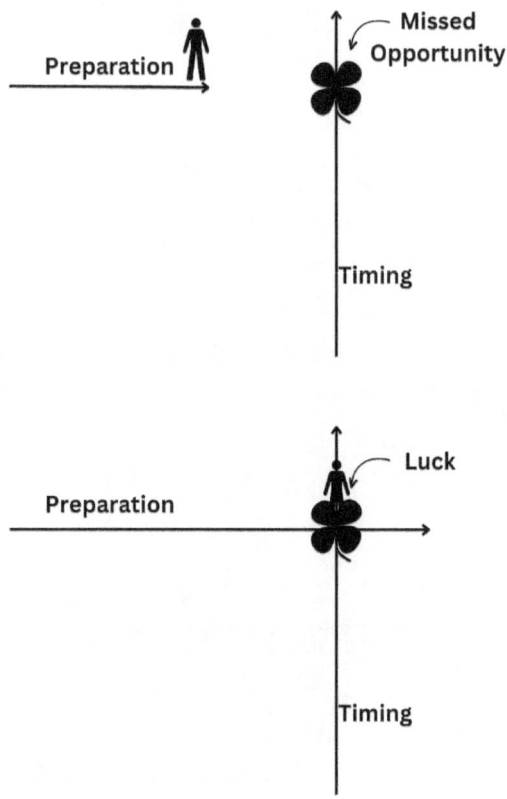

Don't practice until you get it right. Practice until you can't get it wrong: Many people fall into the trap of only practicing something until they have successfully completed the task once. Then, they move on thinking they are ready to utilize that skill in real-life situations. However, this approach falls short in two ways.

First, by practicing until you get it right, you only train your mind and body to execute success one time. Practicing something one time does not provide you with enough repetitions to create a habit or master a skill. While there is no "one size fits all" approach for the number of repetitions required to create a habit or master a skill, one thing is certain: The more you practice, the more likely you are to form a habit of executing it correctly.

The second shortfall is that one successful practice, that occurred in a low-pressure situation, is not representative of real life. It's a low-pressure situation because you have unlimited chances to get it done right. The lack of immediate consequences and the ability to repeat the task until it is done correctly during low-pressure situations does not adequately prepare you for the added stress and pressure you will face in actual life events, which usually do not come with "do-overs."

If you only train your mind to successfully complete a task once in a low-pressure environment, what do you think the outcome will be in a real-life scenario?

To truly prepare and create your own luck, it is essential to practice until you can't get it wrong, regardless of the scenario you are faced with. This way, when faced with a high-pressure situation, your mind is programmed to perform effectively and achieve success.

Put yourself in the shoes of a public speaker for a moment. Simply delivering your speech flawlessly once, even in front of a mirror, may not be enough preparation for the unpredictable nature of a live presentation. Consider how quickly you can be thrown off by an audience member asking a question, despite your request for questions to be held until the end. Plan what you would do in the event of a technical issue, such as a malfunctioning microphone or a computer restart, to keep your audience engaged. Think about what would happen if you forgot your lines. These are all scenarios that can happen during a live presentation, and without proper preparation and practice, they could negatively impact your level of success.

The principle of practicing until you can't get it wrong applies to every aspect of life. A musician must repeatedly practice until their performance is second nature. A cook must be prepared for any kitchen challenges that may arise. A doctor must be well-versed in emergency procedures. A lawyer must be able to argue a case confidently in court no matter what the opposing counsel presents.

Regardless of what you are doing or what you are preparing for, you must keep practicing your craft until it becomes automatic, so that even in high-pressure or unpredictable situations, you are able to perform with ease. This is when your luck will be created.

Socialize

In the chapter, "Silence the Noise," we briefly discussed how building relationships should be your most prioritized investment of time after self-care activities.

Success is often not about what you know but about who you know. People who have a larger network typically have more access to opportunities and resources than those with smaller networks. As a result, people with larger networks seem to be "luckier" and more successful.

Take a moment and think about all the good things you have in life. It could be your job, the products you use, the major you study, or other aspects of your life. More often than not, these opportunities and successes originated from your network of connections and recommendations from people you know.

Making connections and building relationships will open doors that may have been previously closed, leading to a wider range of opportunities. When you interact with others, you gain access to a variety of resources, including knowledge, experiences, and new ideas.

However, what's often overlooked is the indirect benefits of socializing. Every time you connect with someone, you interact not only directly with them, but also indirectly with their entire network! This person becomes a gateway to even more individuals who can open doors for you in ways you may have never imagined. In other words, when you socialize, you aren't just connecting with one person; you are connecting with multiple people.

Additionally, socializing allows you to learn from others and gain a new perspective on life. Don't confuse socializing with always having to talk. The most successful people often speak less and listen more. They actively listen to their counterparts and understand the value of being present in the moment, rather than always having to dominate the conversation. By taking the time to listen and absorb information from others, they are able to gather valuable insights that can contribute to their own success.

Here's the point: The more connections you make, the more doors you're able to walk through, and the greater your chances of success will be. In other words, the larger your network, the more luck you create for yourself.

Building quality relationships can't be done overnight. Think about your relationships with your closest friends, which probably were not formed overnight but through consistent effort over time. With this in mind, start small and take it one day at a time to broaden your network. Here are some steps you can take to begin building new relationships:

- Make it a goal to never eat alone. Sharing a meal with someone can be a great way to build a connection and get to know someone better.
- Engage with others in your community and industry. Attend events, participate in group activities, and join clubs or organizations that align with your interests.
- Rekindle lost connections by reaching out to friends you haven't talked to in a while. Give them a call on your way home from work or during a walk.
- Show kindness and be friendly. Smile, make eye contact, and say hello to everyone you meet.

When you consistently socialize and are prepared with a clear idea of what you want to achieve, it will help you capitalize on opportunities when they arise. Every little bit goes a long way. Over time, as your network grows larger, you will notice more good fortune coming your way.

Remove your emotions

Your emotions, both positive and negative, have the power to significantly turn up the volume on the amount of noise in your life. Your emotions can cloud your judgment and impair your ability to make rational decisions, which often leads to unfavorable outcomes.

Think about these real-life examples where emotions play a huge role. In the phenomenon of stock market bubbles, impulsive investments fueled by greed and fear can have disastrous outcomes. In sports, emotions can distract from a player's focus and lead to missed shots or penalties. In politics, decisions made in the heat of the moment can lead to strained relationships between nations. In your personal finances, impulsive purchases based on emotional desires can lead to high credit card debt and financial instability. Socially, emotions can cause us to say something hurtful to people we care about in the heat of the moment.

Emotional decision-making often misleads people into believing that the outcome was a result of the poor hand they were dealt. However, in reality, it's simply the result of not folding their hands and waiting for their emotions to subside before acting.

Mentally strong and successful people possess a common trait: the ability to regulate their emotions, regardless of the situation. They don't get carried away by highs or overwhelmed by lows.

While it's normal to experience emotions, it's essential to refrain from making big decisions or taking significant actions that are based on, or affected by, those emotions. Making decisions in the heat of the moment often leads to bad outcomes.

Mentally strong people use a common technique known as the 24-hour rule to help regulate emotions and make effective decisions.

The 24-hour rule is a powerful tool for managing emotions and making informed decisions. By waiting 24 hours before acting, you give yourself time for emotions to subside and for a clearer perspective to emerge. For example, Jeff Bezos is known to make important decisions around 10:30 a.m. every morning, after he has had time to think about his choices. By delaying his decision until he's had a chance to sleep on it and allow his emotions to subside, he is able to think things through and avoid making impulsive decisions influenced by emotions.

The 24-hour rule is a simple yet effective way to ensure that your decisions are based on reason, logic, and facts, rather than emotions and impulses.

If you don't have 24 hours, then the simplest and most effective solution is often the one that is most overlooked: breathing. Breathing is something you always have control over. Stepping away from the situation and taking a few deep breaths can go a long way toward regulating your emotions to effectively play the hand you have been dealt.

The longer and deeper you breathe, the better. Numerous studies have shown that slow, deep breathing can activate the parasympathetic nervous system, which is responsible for relaxing your body after periods of stress or danger. By slowing down and controlling your breathing, you can calm the nervous system and reduce emotional intensity.

Meditation is a powerful tool that can help you achieve long, deep breaths that can bring you to a state of equilibrium. It has been proven effective by many successful individuals who incorporate it into their daily routines. For example, consider comments from the following people:

- Ellen DeGeneres, comedian and host of *The Ellen DeGeneres Show*, has said, *"Meditation helps me stay centered, focused, and in the present, which allows me to be a better listener and respond with empathy and purpose."*
- Hugh Jackman, a famous actor, has said, *"Meditation is a tool that helps quiet the mind. That's something we all need in our busy, crazy lives."*
- Arianna Huffington, a co-founder of the Huffington Post, has said, *"Meditation is a huge part of my morning routine. It's like hitting the reset button for my day."*

And if you follow professional sports, you may have noticed an increasing trend among athletes who practice meditation before and during games. This is a testament to the powerful benefits of meditation as a technique for regulating emotions and improving performance.

However, there is still a misunderstanding that meditation is difficult, strange, or limited to sitting in silence. Meditation is much more diverse and accessible than people think. It includes more than just sitting in one place. Moving meditation, such as going for a walk or run, can have a profound impact on regulating your emotions. Countless studies have shown that participating in an aerobic activity can reduce depression, stress, anxiety, and other negative emotions. There are also many apps that offer guided experiences, such as Peloton, Calm, and Apple Fitness. To enhance your meditation experience and fully immerse yourself, try using headphones to block out external distractions and noise.

If none of these options are for you, then try "boxed breathing" as another technique to calm yourself. This technique is easy. Simply close your eyes and visualize drawing a box in your mind. As shown in the visual below, draw each side of the box for *four seconds* as you inhale for one side, hold for the next side, exhale for the next side, and hold for the next side.

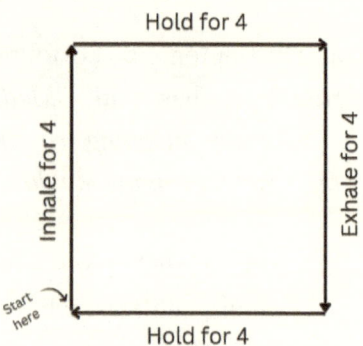

Take a moment and try to perform one round of boxed breathing. Take your time and focus on each inhale, hold, exhale, and hold. Notice how different you feel after completing just one box.

The more boxes you complete, the greater sense of calm you'll feel. It's important not to rush, as the pace of your breathing is key to regulating your emotions. Just breathe, and remember, it's the quality of each breath that counts, not the speed at which you do it. Ultimately, the more effectively you can remove emotions from your decisions and actions, the more luck you will create for yourself in your life.

Resilience and perseverance

The development of resilience and perseverance was thoroughly covered in the previous chapter, but it bears repeating as it plays a crucial role in the creation of luck and ultimately, success. Many people overlook the fact that luck often resides in being able to stay in the game long enough until something breaks in your favor.

Utilize what you learned in the chapter "Develop Resilience and Perseverance" as the final piece in the formula to create your own luck.

Remember, some people want success to happen, and others wish it will happen. But mentally strong people make it happen by creating their own luck. Remind yourself that nobody is going to give it to you. You just have to create it for yourself. If you work on the luck formula and stay in the game long enough, at some point, luck will come your way.

Finally, don't forget the wise words of Benjamin Franklin, one of the Founding Fathers of the United States:

"Failing to prepare, is preparing to fail."

-Benjamin Franklin

TRAIT 6

LEARN HOW TO BE POSITIVE AND OPTIMISTIC

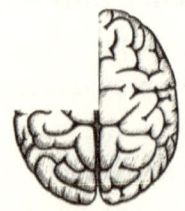

With just one word, let me paint a scenario we have all experienced: heartbreak.

Most people have had their hearts broken at some point in their lives. According to research, over 80% of people have had their hearts broken. In most cases, the causes of heartbreak were romantic in nature. They might have included breakup, infidelity, rejection, or just not being single at the same time as another potential partner.

But it doesn't stop there. There are many other things that can cause heartbreak, such as the loss of a loved one or the loss of a pet. A broken heart can be caused by an acute illness, a major surgery, a broken bone, or the inability to have children. The list goes on and on.

Before we begin, take a moment and think about a time in your life when you had your heart broken. What happened? Who was involved? Bring that to the front of your mind.

Do you still remember the feeling? Do you remember what it felt like a couple of days, weeks, months, and even years after? Does it still cause you pain to this day?

As human beings, we're able to move on (at least in part) from our heartbreaks over time. But in the moment, it feels as if we will never fully heal, and emotional pain takes over our minds.

We start to feel hopeless. We start to feel like life is out to get us. We start to feel depressed. We start to only see the downside in opportunities that come our way. And we subconsciously develop a negative mindset because life has proven these outcomes already.

To cope and heal, many people try therapy, reach out to family and friends, read books, or look for helpful resources online.

With any of these coping mechanisms, there are a few common phrases we are frequently told that will help cure everything. How many times have you heard someone tell you to "be positive," "remain optimistic," "hang in there," "see the glass as half full," or "be grateful for what you have"?

In theory, this advice seems to make sense. But dealing with life's mental challenges is not as simple as flipping a switch anytime someone reminds you to be positive or to remain optimistic. So why doesn't it work?

If you think about the advice more closely, did any of it, or anyone, also *teach* you how to actually *be* positive, stay optimistic, hang in there, see the glass as half full, or be grateful for what you have? Probably not, because it's not that simple.

While the people giving this advice have the best intentions at heart, the fact is most people have not learned how to do it themselves either. Learned positivity and learned optimism is a skill that is developed over time not in an instant.

Think about it. If you wanted to be a teacher, you wouldn't simply teach a course in school that you have not spent countless hours learning about previously. If you wanted to learn how to be a great basketball player, the advice to simply "play basketball" wouldn't be too helpful.

But if I taught you how to dribble, how to pass, how to shoot, how to play defense, how to lift weights, how to eat properly, and how to be a good teammate, you would surely be a much better player.

The same goes for building a positive and optimistic mind. Hearing mantras about being positive and optimistic will only get you so far. Learning how to reshape your mindset and attitude is the key. Consider this comment from Sundar Pichai, CEO of Alphabet and Google, who once said:

"A person who is happy is not happy because everything is right in his life. He is happy because his attitude toward everything in his life is right."

Here's the point: The strongest-minded and successful people understand the importance of maintaining a positive and optimistic attitude. They recognize that this is the golden key to overcoming life's challenges and achieving success. Consider these comments from the following successful people:

- Wade Boggs, a Hall of Fame baseball player, once said, *"A positive attitude causes a chain reaction of positive thoughts, events, and outcomes. It is a catalyst, and it sparks extraordinary results."*
- Pat Riley, a Hall of Fame basketball player and coach, once said, *"If you have a positive attitude and constantly strive to give your best effort, eventually you will overcome your immediate problems and find you are ready for greater challenges."*
- Mary Lou Retton, the gold medal Olympic gymnast, once said, *"Optimism is a happiness magnet. If you stay positive, good things and good people will be drawn to you."*

Ultimately, each successful person mastered the trait of learning *how* to be positive and optimistic. Each person was able to train his or her mind to look at any situation with a positive and optimistic outlook, no matter how dire the situation seemed in the present moment.

So how can you do it? Learning how to be positive and optimistic begins with the fundamental concept of "living in the width."

Live in the width

The most successful people I know are my parents. Despite immigrating from Iran in the 1970s, knowing very little English, and facing countless obstacles, they persevered and achieved incredible success. They came to the United States with very little money but with a determination to provide a better life for their children. They overcame the language barrier and cultural differences, worked tirelessly to build a life for themselves and our family, and sacrificed their own needs to ensure that my brothers and I had happy, comfortable lives.

One cloudy day, my dad and I were driving in the car, and he noticed that I seemed to always be looking ahead to the next big thing in life, constantly stressed and anxious about what the future held. He saw how I had a pattern of obtaining one goal after another but never taking the time to enjoy or appreciate what I had accomplished. He said, *"You always wanted to buy a car. When you finally had enough money to make the purchase, you left the lot and immediately set your sights on buying a house. And once you closed on that house, you immediately set your focus on buying your next house."* He then said, *"What's the point of going through all the struggles and challenges if you don't take time to appreciate the experiences and embrace the surprises that come your way?"*

As we continued driving, he reminded me that, just like the car we were in, life was always moving forward. He said, *"You, just like most people, are always looking forward to the next thing, or looking behind you dwelling on the past. But there is more to life than just looking forward and backward. You also have to remember to look left and right. You have to remember to live in the width."*

He told me to look out the window. As I turned my head left and right, I noticed the beauty of the farmlands and countryside that surrounded us. At that moment, my mindset forever shifted.

Anytime I feel anxious, depressed, or negative, I remember to look left and right and appreciate what I have, not what I don't have or want to have in the future. I instantly feel stronger, regardless of the situation I'm facing.

Living in the width is the mindset that enables you to foster positivity and optimism. The actions you take in the width can have a profound impact on strengthening your sense of positivity and optimism. The ability to look left and right is a key differentiator that separates a positive-minded person from a negative-minded person and a successful person from an unsuccessful person. As Drew Brees, considered to be one of the greatest NFL quarterbacks, once said:

> *"If you are only ever focused on the mountain in the distance, you might trip over the molehill in front of you."*

How to live in the width

Living in the width requires you to be mindful. Mindfulness is a term that's often thrown around in discussions about mental health, mental strength, and well-being, but it often leaves people confused about what it exactly means. Some might equate it with meditation or relaxation techniques, while others see it as a broader philosophy for living.

At its core, mindfulness is about one thing: paying attention to the present moment and being fully engaged in your experiences, rather than dwelling on the past or worrying about the future. Mindfulness is a simple yet powerful concept that has the potential to transform your life and lay the groundwork for becoming a positive and optimistic person.

Think back to your greatest accomplishment in life, the moment that filled you with pride and satisfaction. Maybe it was graduating from college, landing your dream job, starting a family, having children, immigrating to a new country, or overcoming a personal challenge. Whatever it was, you likely worked hard to achieve that dream.

Now ask yourself: After you achieved that milestone, what came next? Did you immediately set your sights on a new goal or dream of something even bigger and more challenging? For instance, after buying your first car, did you start dreaming about owning your first home?

If you're like many people, the answer is probably yes. We're conditioned to constantly strive for more, to never be satisfied with our current accomplishments. We are always rushing to the next thing or dwelling over what just happened. We're always looking forward and backward.

Success does not come from worrying about what happened in the past or what you hope will happen in the future. It comes from being present in the moment and focusing on what you can control.

Eleanor Roosevelt, a prominent activist for civil rights, women's rights, and human rights, and widely regarded as one of the most influential and important women in American history, once said:

"Yesterday is history, tomorrow is a mystery, but right here, right now, is a gift. That's why it's called the present."

As someone who dedicated her life to changing the future for so many people, her recognition of the value of being present serves as a powerful reminder to look left and right, to live in the width, and to appreciate the beauty of your life as it unfolds.

To practice having a positive and optimistic mindset and be fully aware of your present thoughts and emotions, try incorporating the following techniques:

1. Don't say anything to yourself that you wouldn't say to others.
2. Reframe your thoughts with the power of the word "yet".
3. Get on the right bus.
4. Find the silver lining.

Don't say anything to yourself that you wouldn't say to others

Self-talk has a direct impact on your mental health. Self-talk is your inner voice speaking to you, combining conscious thoughts with your beliefs, biases, and personal experiences. Some of this self-talk may come from facts, logic, and reason. But other self-talk may be derived from your own misconceptions about a situation, fears, and disproportionate negative filtering.

Negative filtering is an inherent flaw in human nature. Everyone experiences it at some point in their lives, some more commonly than others. Negative filtering occurs when you filter out all or most of the positive information about a situation and only allow the negative information to flow through. Negative filtering occurs when you automatically anticipate the worst possible thing that could happen, without considering the fact that it's highly unlikely to happen. Negative filtering occurs when you only consider two drastic sides of the spectrum, the good and the bad, and there is no possibility of a middle ground.

As you disproportionately allow negative information to replace positive information, you continue to weaken your mind.

A common situation where this occurs is with the fear of flying. Depending on the research statistic you look at, upwards of 60% of the population has some fear of flying, ranging from slight anxiety to full-blown terror.

The fear of flying can keep people from going on their dream vacations, traveling to see family members, and saying no to potentially life-changing opportunities. Ultimately, this fear prevents those people from achieving all they are capable of.

Most people, even those with a fear of flying, know that flying is one of the safest forms of travel. It's safer than driving a car and even sleeping in your own bed at night, and it is only getting safer.

The Federal Aviation Administration, in cooperation with world-class statistician Arnold Barnett from the Massachusetts Institute of Technology (MIT), published the following statistics showing plane crashes on commercial flights:

- 1968-1977: one death per 350,000 commercial boardings.
- 1978-1987: one death per 750,000 commercial boardings.
- 1988-1997: one death per 1.3 million commercial boardings.
- 1998-2007: one death per 2.7 million commercial boardings.
- 2008-2017: one death per 7.9 million commercial boardings.
- And as of 2023: one death per 14.3 million commercial boardings.

In other words, you have a 99.99999% chance of getting to your destination safely. So why do over 60% of people have some form of flight anxiety when almost all flights land safely? What is causing this disproportion? It is the prevalence of negative filtering in a person's mind.

In this situation, negative filtering occurs because people only visualize what can go wrong. They visualize the plane crashing, severe turbulence, or the pilot losing control.

These people forget to look around, account for the *facts*, and remember that positive things are much more likely to happen. They forget that essentially all commercial flights land safely. They forget that being on the plane will give them some extra time to take a nap, read a book, or catch up on their favorite show. They forget about the positive experience they will have at their destination.

If these people were able to proportionally filter all thoughts, both positive and negative, they would be able to achieve levels of success they previously thought were impossible.

Ironically, when these people are not flying, they are often the first to reassure others who are afraid to fly that flying is one of the safest modes of transportation. They will encourage others to get on the plane. The reason is, as human beings, we tend to be harder on ourselves than we are on other people.

To put this in perspective, think about the last time others close to you seemed to be struggling. When you noticed they were struggling, what did you say to them? You probably gave them advice on what they should and shouldn't be doing to navigate through their challenges. Most importantly, you likely reduced or eliminated the amount of negative communication directed toward them.

It's this example alone that proves we "know" what needs to be done to work through our very own challenges. Yet when we are faced with a similar challenge ourselves, we often skip this same advice and instead tell ourselves something that we would never think of saying to someone close to us.

This leads to the technique that will instantly improve your positive thinking. *Don't say anything to yourself that you wouldn't say to other people.*

Mentally strong people know not to say anything to themselves that they wouldn't say to others going through the same situation. Consider this quote from Lisa M. Hayes, which has since been repeated many times over by many other successful individuals:

"Be careful how you are talking to yourself because you are listening."

Living in the width provides you an opportunity to be conscious of your own self-talk and aware of how you filter information in your mind.

The next time you encounter a challenge or a negative thought creeps into your head, pause for a moment and reflect on how your self-talk and filtering may be contributing to negative thinking before you consider giving up. This moment of mindfulness presents an opportunity to filter back in positive thinking and shift your mindset toward positivity.

Ask yourself if you would say the same thing to someone else going through the exact same situation. If the answer is no, then tell yourself what you *would* tell someone else.

This technique can have a profound impact on your mental state, mental strength, and ability to conquer all that life throws your way.

Reframe with the power of the word "yet"

It is possible to learn how to turn negative thinking, negative self-talk, and negative filtering into positive filtering, positive self-talk, and positive thinking. It begins with reframing a situation.

Reframing is a technique to shift your mindset about a particular situation you are facing. It involves looking at the current situation and expanding on the possible outcomes and possibilities. In other words, it involves looking at a particular situation from a different angle.

Reframing is something you can do anywhere, anytime you are experiencing a negative thought. The outcome of reframing will change the way you think and feel.

There are many ways you can reframe a particular situation. However, the simplest way involves just one word: "yet."

It's amazing how a single word can have such a profound impact on your mindset. When you reframe a negative situation with the word "yet", the situation turns from something that seemed to be final, into a situation that only presently exists.

The word "yet" is like a vehicle waiting to take you on a journey to a better future. This small shift in perspective creates an opportunity for you to hit the open road and drive on the "highways" of change, taking you from a negative location to a more positive place. Observe how the outlook on similar situations drastically changes with the word "yet":

NEGATIVE MINDSET　　**POSITIVE MINDSET**

- I can't do the job
- I'm not strong enough
- I can't function after the breakup　　**...yet**
- I don't have enough money
- My child won't listen to me
- I can't fly on an airplane

Adding the word "yet" is a powerful tool. But solely having a car will not get you to your destination. You still need to drive it on the roads that lead to your desired destination. Getting to your destination involves having a plan. To put this in perspective, consider these examples:

- If your destination is to start a successful business, you must create a plan of what the business will look like, what products or services you'll provide, and what budget you'll be working with.
- If your destination is to live a healthier lifestyle, you must create a plan for daily eating habits and exercise.
- If your destination is to pay for your child's education, you must create a plan to budget and save money.

- If your destination is to have a wedding, you must plan when and where it will be, who will be invited, and how much you want to spend.

Your plan to your destination is unique to you. Consider the journey of a road trip. Even those who love road trips often find that they are long, unfamiliar, tiring, and uncomfortable at times. These days, most people wouldn't go on a road trip without using a GPS. A GPS will provide you with several options for getting to your destination. Some options are faster, some are cheaper, and some are more fuel-efficient. But no matter what, your route will be different from others who are starting their road trips from different locations.

The point is, in life there is no "one size fits all" approach to get to your destination. Even if your destination is the same as someone else's, you are likely starting from different points. Just because others have what you want or are where you want to be, does not mean you will take the same path and amount of time that they did to get there. Just because someone is already at your destination, you should not be discouraged from continuing to try and get there yourself.

To help get to your destination, try adding "in order to" and a three-step plan following the word "yet". The steps of your plan symbolize the roads to your destination. While you can add as many steps to your plan as you want, it's best to keep it limited to three specific items that are attainable for you. For example, consider a person who recently started a new job. There is always a learning curve with starting a new job. It can be overwhelming to learn and address all of the responsibilities of the job simultaneously. It doesn't matter if you are the lowest-ranking employee or the CEO. It is natural to doubt yourself at times and think, "I can't do this job." But this is not a positive or productive mindset.

Instead, mentally strong people shift their mindsets from "I can't do the job," to "I can't do the job yet," to "I can't do the job yet. In order to do the job, I need to:

1. be willing to reach out to others for help and ask questions,
2. be comfortable communicating that I do not know all the answers, and
3. be willing to put in extra hours until I get more acclimated to the role."

Here, the destination is clear and so is the plan to get there. It is now on the individual to execute that plan and begin the "drive" on the road trip.

However, it's important to remember that no matter how much you plan, no plan will ever be 100% perfect. When you use GPS on a road trip, you still might make a wrong turn. There might be unexpected traffic along the way. You'll have to stop for gas. You'll probably get to your destination at a different time than originally planned. But no matter what you encounter along the way, your GPS will always recalculate and adjust your plan to get you to your destination. The GPS is resilient and always perseveres.

This is how mentally strong and successful people navigate the challenging roads in life. Even if they make a wrong turn or realize they are headed in the wrong direction, they do not stop. Instead, they consistently pivot and change their plans in order to get to their destination. They stay resilient and persevere using the techniques you already learned in the chapter, "Develop Resilience and Perseverance."

If part of your plan isn't working or you feel lost along the way, you must learn to simply adjust your plan, adjust your steps in real-time, and pivot to get you to your destination.

Before moving on to the next section, take a moment to think about what is most challenging to you right now. Can you add the word "yet" to the end of that thought process? Where is it that you want to go? What's your destination? It can be as simple as "being happier."

Can you create an initial three-step plan to help you work through any negative thought process and start working toward your positive destination?

Once you define your three-step plan, it is now on you to follow through with it. As you work through your plan, you might realize that one or even all three of the items you defined are not working. Don't hesitate to reevaluate and change your route to get you to your destination.

Get on the right bus

You might've heard the phrase, *"You are the combination of the five people you spend the most time with."* The meaning behind this phrase is simple. Our personalities and mindsets are pieced together over time using the traits and personalities we like and dislike from the people closest to us. At first, it comes from parents and siblings, then friends, family, co-workers, and even enemies. Your personality and mindset are molded into a blend of these very people in your life.

No matter how much you try, your mindset is *dependent* on the people you surround yourself with most frequently. What these people do affects what you do, whether you realize it or not. This is why most people who are great at their crafts also had great mentors, teachers, and teams that they learned from along the way. Consider this comment from Mike Krzyzewski. He said:

> *"The **best advice I ever got** throughout my whole life was when I was 14. The night before my first day of high school my mom said, 'Make sure you get on the right bus.'*

> *"At that time, I was a 14-year-old wise guy and I replied, 'Mom, I know the city.' My mom's response was, 'That's not the bus I'm talking about.' I asked, 'What bus do you mean?'*

> *"She answered, 'The bus you are going to drive for the rest of your life. Only put good people on that bus. And only get on a bus that's driven by a good person. Because you'll never accomplish what you want by doing it alone, but you'll accomplish a heck of a lot more by doing it with great people.'"*

Ultimately, people come into your life for one of four reasons: to add, subtract, multiply, or divide. It's no different for building a strong positive mind. Fill your bus with more positive-minded people and the more positive you will become. Fill it with more negative-minded people and the more negative you will become.

Let's take a moment and assess what bus you are currently riding. Start with the five people you surround yourself with most frequently. These are your multipliers and dividers. Their impact on you is more influential than others in your life. Think about their mindsets. Are they generally positive or negative? Place the names of the individuals with positive mindsets in the "multiply" window of the bus. Place the names of the individuals with negative mindsets in the "divide" window of the bus.

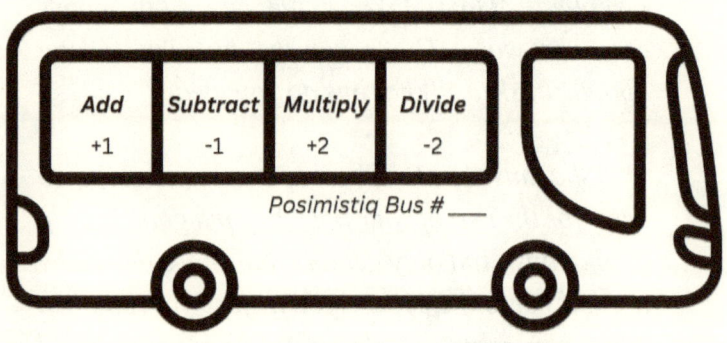

Then, think about anyone else you interact with on a consistent basis, such as friends, family, or coworkers. These individuals are your adders and subtractors. While their impact may not be as great as your multipliers and dividers, they still play a role in shaping your mindset. Place the names of the individuals with positive mindsets in the "add" window of the bus. Place the names of the individuals with negative mindsets in the "subtract" window of the bus.

To determine your overall score, tally up the names in each window and assign values accordingly. The multipliers receive a value of *two*, dividers receive a value of *negative two*, adders receive a value of *one*, and subtractors receive a value of *negative one*. What bus number are you currently riding? Is it positive or negative?

Regardless of your current bus number, your goal now is to start thinking about who is on your bus and what steps you can take to increase your bus number by surrounding yourself with more positive-minded people.

Over time, you should look to identify others who you believe have a positive mindset. If you can, bring them on to your bus, spend more time with them, and learn from them. Conversely, removing negative-minded people from your bus can also increase your bus number.

This does not mean you need to cut every negative person out of your life. Relationships are complicated and each person is in your life for a reason. But simply setting boundaries with those that are negative and increasing your time spent with those that are positive, will help you naturally build your positive mindset and see the world differently.

Now, you may be thinking, "I don't know anyone that I can bring on my bus." That is okay! Many of us are in this position.

Increasing the concentration of positivity in your life does not have to occur just through the people that you know. There are other things you can do to increase the concentration of positivity in your life. For example, on social media, you can look for and follow accounts specifically focused on positivity and happiness. You can also unfollow accounts that make you feel inadequate, make you feel like you're missing out on something, or otherwise have a negative vibe to them. Consider the types of television shows and movies you watch and the characters that are portrayed in these shows. Is there an opportunity for you to improve what you're watching? You can search for positivity videos or motivational speakers on the internet and watch these speeches from time to time. There's amazing content on TED Talks and MasterClass for helping to build stronger minds. All of these things can be added to your bus.

The point is, you can seek out positivity connections in anything you do daily, from shows and videos you watch, to books you read. Bring them onto your bus. There is only so much negativity you can allow in your life before it consumes you. The right people and content will help shape your mind and help you stay positive.

Find the silver lining

To increase your positive thought process, one technique is to always find a "silver lining" in a situation, no matter what you are going through. A silver lining is a sign of hope or a positive aspect in an otherwise negative situation. The phrase is often seen as part of the proverb, "Every cloud has a silver lining," meaning there is hope or something good to be found in every bad situation. In real life, when a cloud looks like its edges are shiny and silvery, it's because the sun is behind it.

That is the metaphor. Things are cloudy (negative), but they will get sunny (positive) again. And while things are bad, there is usually at least one shiny (positive) part in all the gloominess.

There is always a hidden blessing and always something positive to be gained from a negative situation. You just have to look for it and find it. If this sounds familiar, it's because this thought process is similar to the reframing technique. For example:

- Getting your wisdom teeth out is painful, but a silver lining is you get to eat a lot of ice cream after.
- Losing your job is scary, but a silver lining is you're free to find a job more aligned with your passions.
- Breaking up with your significant other always hurts, but a silver lining is that you now have more time to yourself.
- Going through any challenge is always difficult, but a silver lining is you will learn from the experience and be mentally stronger once it's over.

Sometimes, the silver lining in difficult situations is as simple as being grateful for what you already have. It's important to remember that what you perceive as a problem may not necessarily be a problem in the grand scheme of things.

To put this in perspective, people tend to always want more when they are healthy, but when they become sick, they realize that their health is the one thing that truly matters.

Think back to the last time you were really sick. What was the one thing you wanted more than anything else? Most likely, it was simply to not be sick anymore. This serves as a powerful reminder of the value of your health and the importance of being grateful for it.

If you have a roof over your head, access to clean water and food, or a supportive network of friends and family, be grateful for that. Imagine how you would feel if any of these were taken away from you. These are the little silver linings that you can be grateful for, regardless of what your situation is.

It's also crucial to maintain a clear perspective. Your environment can easily skew your perception and lead you to negativity, particularly when you compare yourself to others around you.

However, stepping outside of your usual environment and into a different community can help you recalibrate your vision and cultivate a more positive mindset. For example, visiting a less affluent neighborhood can provide a powerful reminder of the things you may take for granted. By gaining a fresh perspective, you can shift your focus from what you lack to what you have.

If it sounds too difficult to find the silver lining, you're skeptical about the approach, or you think your situation is too dark to have any silver linings, consider the story of Eric Legrand.

Eric Legrand was a Rutgers University football player who became paralyzed after making a tackle in a game on October 16, 2010. It's hard to imagine many scenarios that would be more challenging than what occurred to him on that day. Yet, through all difficulties in his journey, he has said:

> *"My life changed in an instant, but I will never look back and wonder 'what if' because I have been blessed with an opportunity to make a difference – to inspire the world – for all individuals no matter their ability."*
>
> *-Eric LeGrand*

If he can find a silver lining, you can too.

TRAIT 7

TAKE CARE OF YOUR GRASS

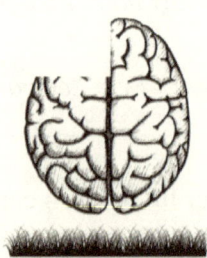

You are probably familiar with the well-known proverb, "The grass is always greener on the other side." Typically, the proverb means that even though someone else's situation seems better, it is usually not as good as it appears.

Despite this well-known proverb, many people continue to compare their own lives to those of others, believing that they would be happier or more successful if they had something different. Ironically, it's this very thought process that is making them unhappy and mentally weak.

It's in these everyday moments where weak-minded people make life decisions such as changing jobs, homes, lifestyles, and habits. They think each decision will be the one that makes their lives as green as the situation or person they envy. But those same people often end up in the same position as they were previously, looking over the fence, unhappy and unsatisfied with their lawn color.

Here's a little secret: The proverb, as stated above, is incomplete. Mentally strong and successful people shift their focus and change the proverb to read:

The grass is always greener on the other side
<u>if it is taken care of.</u>

If you want to be mentally strong and successful, then you must take care of your grass. You may be wondering: How do I take care of my grass? At a high level, it is no different than the eight major components of lawn care maintenance. Each component works in harmony and is vital in the ability to grow, reproduce, survive, and achieve the outcome you strive for. To keep your grass healthy, you need soil, seeds, water, fertilizer, and sunlight. You need to treat the weeds, diseases, and insects. You need to cut the grass from time to time. Taking care of your "mind's grass" is no different. It takes time, care, commitment, and the right balance of all components.

As we walk through each component of taking care of your "mind's grass," you will begin to recognize how each of the components of lawn care maintenance can be applied to building mental strength.

The next time you are faced with a difficult situation, you'll have a choice in the way you react. You can choose to react in a way that holds you back, or you can choose to react in a way that propels you forward.

Weak-minded people react in a way that holds them back by assuming the grass is greener on the other side. However, strong-minded people react in a way that propels them forward by knowing the grass is greener only if it is taken care of. Which type of person do you want to be?

Soil = set your foundation

The strength of grass often depends on what is below the surface. Below the surface is where the roots grow. The roots create the strong foundation that enables the grass to thrive and survive no matter the conditions it is put through. There is no amount of water, sunlight, or seeds that will strengthen a lawn if the soil below the surface is poor.

The same goes for building mental strength. There is no amount of practice that will build sustained mental strength if your foundation below the surface is weak. A strong foundation creates a strong root system that keeps you grounded, regardless of the adversity you face.

To understand how to build a strong foundation, consider this quote from Mark Wahlberg, a successful actor and producer who has overcome numerous challenges in his life, who has said:

"Recognize that life isn't supposed to be easy. There are no handouts or entitlements. You must keep going and keep working. Don't expect someone else to figure it out for you."

Your foundation will strengthen with what you have already learned throughout this book, which includes:

- The willingness to be vulnerable.
- Having a purpose.

- The ability to silence the noise.
- Being committed for the long haul, and recognizing that failure is part of any process. Success takes grit, perseverance, and patience.
- The willingness to create your own luck.
- Having a positive and optimistic mindset.

These attributes will enhance the quality of your thoughts and create a strong foundation to allow you to handle any challenge that comes your way.

Seeds = plant your commitments

Once your foundation is set, it is ready to support whatever seed you plant. Mental strength and success come in many different forms, just as there are many types of grass seeds to choose from. Think about what you want your product to look like and pick your seed accordingly.

What do you want to change in your life? What do you want to improve? What type of person do you want to become? The answers to these questions will lead you to your seeds.

Once you know which seeds you want to plant, you must commit to nurturing them. The difference between strong-minded people and weak-minded people is that strong-minded people understand that healthy grass does not grow immediately after the seeds are planted. It takes time. Just as consistent management is vital to a lawn's ability to reproduce, thrive, and survive, the same goes for building mental strength and having success. As Dwayne "The Rock" Johnson has said:

"Success is not overnight. It's when every day you get a little better than the day before. It all adds up."

Water = the "learning never ends" mindset

Most people know that water is crucial in managing a lawn. Watering your lawn regularly is the most important step for grass to grow. Water contributes to stronger roots and provides the best opportunity to have a strong, healthy green lawn.

A "learning never ends" mindset can be compared to watering a lawn. Many people think their learning journey ends after graduation or outside of the classroom. This is nothing more than a tragic flaw in the human mind. A person who fails to continually learn will weaken with time because the world is always changing in profound ways. If you're not willing to be a lifelong learner, it is going to be nearly impossible to keep pace with those around you.

Mentally strong and successful people know that learning never ends. They continue to learn and always seek to improve their knowledge, which allows them to continue to build mental strength. They strive to be a "learn-it-all," not a "know-it-all."

Consider Jeff Bezos, the founder of Amazon, which is one of the most successful businesses in the world. Bezos has always been a voraciously inquisitive learner. He often compares Amazon's strategy of developing ideas in new markets to "planting seeds." He has said:

The Posimistiq Mind

*"Many efforts turn out to be dead ends, but
every once in a while, you go down an alley and it
opens up into this huge, broad avenue."*

Amazon, for instance, didn't begin as a brilliant vision. It began as a business to sell books online. It was only through the learning and discovery process that Bezos led himself to a series of small discoveries, unlocked a revolutionary business model, and enabled Amazon to grow into one of the strongest and biggest businesses worldwide. It makes sense why one of Amazon's leadership principles is to learn and be curious.

So why not make it your goal to have a discovery mentality, to always be curious, and to be willing to learn new things? You never know which doors will open for you just by learning, or trying to learn, new things.

One technique that you can use to help you on your mental strength journey is to live by the 8% goal. The 8% goal is when you dedicate 8% of your time to discovery and learning. Eight percent is the equivalent of about two hours in your day. While two hours may seem like a lot in a single day, it has the potential to yield sky-high benefits and will allow you to consistently accomplish your goals.

Remember, every person in the world, regardless of his or her mental strength, is playing on the same "time" field. We all have 24 hours in a day. However, those that find a way to carve out at least two hours daily for learning and discovery can and will build more mental strength than those who do not. In a way, they are carving out time to water their own grass.

If you are feeling overwhelmed at the thought of this time commitment, remember that learning can be accomplished in many different forms. Reading, listening, watching, and discussing with other people are all opportunities to learn.

Remember that learning doesn't always have to be formal or structured. Often the best way to learn is by trying something new. When was the last time you did something for the first time? If it's been a while, then seize the opportunity to try something new right now. Whether it's a new hobby, skill, or experience, you never know what opportunities for learning might arise from taking a leap and trying something different.

Everything that you do contains a learning opportunity, so always try to take something away from it. Even slight shifts in what you do daily can help achieve this goal. For example, while you are cleaning the house, cutting the lawn, or commuting to work, you can simultaneously listen to a podcast or audiobook as opposed to listening to the same songs over and over again.

Or consider what Stephen Covey, author of *The 7 Habits of Highly Effective People*, famously wrote:

> *"First seek to understand, then be understood."*

This quote emphasizes the importance of listening to and understanding others' perspectives before trying to make them understand your own. By speaking less and listening more, you can adopt a "learn-it-all" mindset instead of a "know-it-all" one. When you listen to others, you open yourself up to new ideas and perspectives that you may not have otherwise considered. It's important to remember that you already know what's in your head, but by actively seeking out the insights of others, you can expand your knowledge and understanding. It's a technique to chip away at the 8% goal.

You have endless opportunities in your day to build in learning blocks. You just have to be creative enough to look for it and be willing to slightly adjust your lifestyle to accommodate it.

Now, don't be fooled. The 8% goal may not be achievable every day. Life is filled with unplanned or unforeseen events. Even successful people fail to reach this goal every day.

The key is to keep the 8% goal in mind every day. Whether you're spending 2%, 4%, 6%, or some other amount of time on learning, the emphasis of the goal is on actively seeking out opportunities for growth and being open to new information. The most important thing is to make progress toward your learning goals and aim to learn at least one new thing every day, no matter how small.

When you have a long-term commitment to learning, a little bit in the short term will amount to a lot in the long run. Don't underestimate how these smaller choices and adjustments, which allow you to learn, will add up over time to form the strongest mind.

When you're learning, you can experience the most growth. The moment you stop learning is when you stop growing, just as grass stops growing when it no longer receives water.

Fertilize = self-care

A healthy lawn needs fertilizer almost as much as it needs water. Over time, the soil uses three important nutrients (potassium, phosphorous, and nitrogen) to produce a lush, green lawn. Fertilizer replenishes these essential nutrients to support future growth and development.

Your life is no different. To flourish, you need to supplement your life with mental-strength fertilizer to replenish what you lose every day. Mental-strength fertilizer is all about self-care.

While weak-minded people think they do not have enough time for self-care, mentally strong people recognize that self-care is not selfish. They prioritize time in their lives for this. Mentally strong and successful people know they need to take care of themselves first, so they can give more to others.

Effective self-care is broken down into three techniques, each replenishing the essential mental strength elements you use every day.

1) Sleep to replenish brain function.
2) Exercise to replenish feel-good endorphins.
3) Nutrition to replenish energy.

Sleep: You may have heard the stories of successful people who pride themselves on how little sleep they get or how they think sleep is for the weak. But most successful and mentally strong people see through this fallacy and realize this is just a narrative that makes for a good story.

Have you heard of the saying "woke up on the wrong side of the bed"? Well, there is truth to it because sleep is closely connected to mental and emotional health.

Not only is there a direct correlation between the amount of sleep you get and the quality of your decision-making and productivity, but there is also a direct correlation between sleep and your mood. Lack of sleep impacts your ability to process positive emotional content. To put this in perspective, some studies show that 75% of depressed people show symptoms of insomnia.

The sweet spot of the exact amount of sleep varies by person, but most people need to get seven to eight hours of sleep per night to refresh their minds, think sharply, and remain upbeat. Even Jeff Bezos aims to get eight hours of sleep most nights. When asked why, he said:

> *"I think better. I have more energy. My mood*
> *is better."*

In other words, it directly impacts his brain function. But the list doesn't stop there. For example, Bill Gates, the founder of Microsoft, has said:

> *"I like to get seven hours of sleep a night*
> *because that is what I need to stay sharp, creative,*
> *and upbeat."*

If you want to feel better, think better, and live better, you need to prioritize consistently getting enough high-quality sleep.

If you're struggling to get enough sleep, try shifting your mindset. Many people think of waking up as the start of their day and going to sleep as the end, but research shows that we're more likely to follow through on tasks that come at the beginning of a sequence rather than the end. For example, when you have a list of errands to run, you're more likely to complete the ones at the beginning of the list than the ones at the end.

Rather than considering sleep as the final task of your day, try shifting your perspective and think of your bedtime routine as the beginning of your day. This mindset can help you prioritize getting enough sleep and maintaining a regular sleep schedule.

Exercise: Exercise can enhance your physique, improve physical performance, and even add years to your life. However, none of these are the main factors motivating mentally strong and successful people to remain active every day.

Have you heard of the saying, "Movement is medicine"? Movement allows you to work on your emotions and reclaim your energy.

Studies show consistent exercise has a profound positive impact on many mental health challenges including depression, anxiety, and stress. This is due to the release of endorphins during exercise, which can provide an energizing, calming, and mood-boosting effect.

Movement also provides you with the brain boosts needed to strengthen your creativity, sharpen your memory, and improve your self-esteem.

The best part about all of this is you don't need to be a star athlete, commit significant amounts of time, or suffer through intense workouts to reap all these benefits that build a stronger mind.

The Centers for Disease Control and Prevention (CDC) recommends 150 minutes of moderate physical activity per week. To put this into perspective, that's only 1.5% of the total minutes in a week, and you can break this down into smaller chunks throughout the week. For example, 30 minutes of moderate exercise five days a week is enough to reap the mental strength benefits, *if you stick with it over the long term.*

Moderate exercise includes a wide range of activities and can be as simple as a walk outside. The point is to get your body moving. Yardwork, cleaning your home, and washing your car are all types of moderate movement that can replenish the feel-good endorphins needed to build a stronger mind.

Many people find it easy to make excuses for not exercising, such as being too busy or having too much work to do. However, rather than viewing exercise as time away from work, consider it as a way to boost your brain power.

Breaking away from work to exercise can be challenging, but even short bursts of movement, like a ten-minute walk, push-ups, or climbing stairs, can enhance creativity and focus.

Sitting for prolonged periods can lead to a reduction in blood flow to the brain. In contrast, physical movement increases blood flow and delivers oxygen and glucose to the brain, which is particularly critical for the prefrontal cortex, the area of the brain involved in problem-solving and decision-making. Incorporating exercise into your daily routine helps to improve your productivity and overall cognitive function, leading to success.

If you can't find time in your day to carve out exercise, then find a way to get creative within your day. For example, take the stairs instead of the elevator. Park further away in the parking lot so you can get more steps in. Every bit of movement adds up.

Ultimately, mentally strong and successful people do not view exercise as a chore. Instead, they associate it as a technique they prioritize on their journey to replenish those feel-good endorphins, build mental strength, boost productivity, and achieve success. They know a regular movement routine will help them develop the mindset needed to achieve whatever seems to be out of reach.

There is no "one size fits all" approach to exercise. Successful people exercise in different ways, and you can too. Consider these examples:

- Richard Branson, the founder of Virgin Group, exercises almost every morning. He prefers swimming and tennis and has claimed he gets upwards of four hours of additional productivity every day by keeping up with his consistent exercise schedule.
- Oprah Winfrey, best known for her talk show, has said, *"I try to do something every day that allows me to feel active."* Some of her preferred forms of exercise are yoga or walking 10,000 steps a day.
- Barack Obama, the 44th President of the United States, exercises 45 minutes per day, six days a week. Weightlifting and cardio are some of his preferred forms of exercise.
- Tim Cook, the CEO of Apple, works out several times a week. Cycling and rock climbing are some of his preferred forms of exercise.

- Mark Cuban, billionaire and owner of the Dallas Mavericks, performs an hour of cardio almost every day. Elliptical, stair master, basketball, and kickboxing are some of his preferred forms of exercise.
- Mark Zuckerberg, the founder of Facebook, exercises at least three days per week. Taking his dog for a run is one of his preferred forms of exercise.

Identify what you enjoy doing, set reasonable goals, and strive to achieve those goals over the long term. If you do this consistently, then you will replenish your body with feel-good endorphins needed to build mental strength and succeed in everyday life.

Nutrition: Your brain is always working, even while you sleep. Therefore, your brain requires a supply of fuel to keep it going.

The way you supply fuel to your brain is through the foods and liquids that you consume throughout the day. But even a race car can only operate at peak performance when it is filled with premium fuel. Therefore, with so many food choices and diets to choose from, it is critical that you supply your brain with a higher concentration of quality foods and liquids.

A mentally strong person knows what they do and don't put into their body directly impacts the functions of their brain and even their mood. Consider these comments from the following successful people:

- Tim Cook, CEO of Apple, said, *"Eating nutritious food is the foundation of a healthy body and mind."*
- Mark Hyman, physician, founder of The UltraWellness Center, and bestselling author of *The UltraMind Solution*, said, *"You can't outrun a bad diet."*
- Ann Wigmore, founder of Hippocrates Health Institute in Boston, said, *"The food you eat can either be the safest and most powerful form of medicine, or the slowest form of poison."*

To put this in perspective, studies show the risk of depression is 25-35% lower in people who consume "traditional" diets, such as the Mediterranean or Japanese diet, compared to those who consume a "Western" diet. This is because traditional diets have a higher concentration of fruits, vegetables, seafood, lean meats, and unprocessed foods, while Western diets have a higher concentration of processed foods, sugar, and fatty meats.

To be clear, this doesn't mean you can't indulge in foods that are tasty and of lower quality. Life is to be enjoyed, and these types of foods are usually the most enjoyable in life. Mentally strong and successful people still eat cookies, ice cream, chips, and other foods that are considered low quality. Some even do it every day.

The difference is that mentally strong people indulge in moderation, all while ensuring they still consume a higher concentration of the highest quality foods over the long term.

In other words, it's about *concentrated balance*. It is not about depriving yourself completely of things you want and crave. Crash diets are not sustainable over the long term.

Instead, a technique you can use to nourish your brain is the 80/20 rule. It's simple: Aim to make 80% of your diet consist of high-quality foods and liquids, while allowing yourself the freedom to indulge in the remaining 20% with the foods that bring you joy or satisfy your cravings.

High-quality foods are typically rich in essential nutrients, including vitamins, minerals, and other beneficial compounds. For example:

- **Fresh fruits and vegetables:** These provide a wealth of fiber, antioxidants, vitamins, and minerals that are vital to maintaining good health.
- **Whole grains:** These include brown rice, whole wheat bread, quinoa, and oats. They offer a rich source of dietary fiber, B vitamins, and other important nutrients that are essential for optimal health.
- **Lean proteins:** Chicken, fish, turkey, eggs, beans, and lentils are all excellent sources of lean protein, which is vital for building and repairing tissues and maintaining a healthy immune system.
- **Nuts and seeds:** These provide healthy fats, fiber, and protein, and are an excellent snack option.
- **Dairy products:** Milk, yogurt, and cheese are all rich in calcium, which is essential for healthy bones, as well as protein and other important nutrients.

- **Healthy fats:** Olive oil and avocado are examples of healthy fats that are beneficial for heart health and can help lower cholesterol levels.

If you consume three main meals a day - breakfast, lunch, and dinner - along with one snack and a dessert, you will be eating a total of five times a day. If you choose to keep your meals and snack in line with the options listed above, then 80% (or four out of five) of your food intake will consist of nutritious and high-quality foods. This leaves room for indulging in dessert or satisfying your cravings, making up the remaining 20% of your food intake.

To be clear, by no means is this an exhaustive list of the only items you can eat. It just gives you an idea of high-quality food options you can consume on your goal to 80%. The main takeaway is that your goal should be to consume 80% high-quality fuels. The remaining 20% can be whatever you desire.

In addition to food, mentally strong people *maximize*, *optimize*, and *minimize* the three most common liquids that impact mental strength and health the most: water, caffeine, and alcohol. They maximize water intake, optimize caffeine intake, and minimize alcohol intake.

Maximize water: Leonardo da Vinci, the famous painter best known for his painting of the *Mona Lisa*, once said:

"Water is the driving force of all nature."

This quote implies that water is the fundamental force that powers and sustains life on Earth. For example, did you know your brain consists of 73% water? No wonder water consumption and brain performance are directly correlated.

Of all the nutritional techniques referenced thus far, maximizing water intake is the one you should strictly adhere to because of how critical it is for your brain to perform optimally. It's far more important to the body and mind than food.

Think about it. A person can only survive about three days without water but can survive significantly longer, sometimes several weeks, without food.

When you don't drink enough water, your brain functions at a lower level. Your memory, focus, attention, and processing of information are all negatively impacted. Studies also show that people who don't drink enough water are at higher risk of depression, anxiety, and stress.

Drinking more water increases blood flow and oxygen to the brain, which carry nutrients to the brain that help brain cells communicate with each other. Ultimately, this leads to improved concentration and memory and enables you to think faster, be more creative, think more clearly, and have increased feelings of relaxation (i.e., reduced stress).

To maximize your water intake to build mental strength, incorporate the following three techniques into your daily routine:

1. *Drink 8-12 ounces of water every morning.* This is the most critical and is non-negotiable. You likely just spent the last third of your day sleeping without a sip of water.

Replenishing your body the moment you wake up will energize you, boost mental performance, and set you up for success each day.

2. *Tie it into a routine.* There are several ways to do this. Before every meal or snack, drink eight ounces of water. Every time you get in the car, take a bottle of water with you. Every time you sit down to relax, drink a glass of water.

3. *Get creative.*

   a. You can increase your water intake not just by drinking water but also by eating foods, such as watermelons, cucumbers, and celery, that have a high water concentration.

   b. Add fruit to your glass of water to flavor it and make it less "boring."

Some studies recommend 124 ounces of water per day for men and 92 ounces of water per day for women. But there is no one-size-fits-all approach. There are so many variables that drive optimal water intake per person such as age, size, health, and level of activity. The rule of thumb for optimal water intake is, "When in doubt, just drink more." You can't really overdo it.

Optimize caffeine: Caffeine can increase your cognitive performance, energy, and alertness. However, overuse can contribute to increased feelings of anxiety, panic, and insomnia.

This is not about denying you your favorite cup of coffee or tea. Plenty of mentally strong people drink caffeine daily. But they are also aware that too much caffeine can negatively impact their mental health, so they monitor the amount they consume. In other words, they *optimize* the impact of caffeine on the brain.

To optimize your caffeine intake and minimize any negative impacts but also reap the benefits of caffeine, you can follow this general rule of thumb:

- Delay having your caffeinated beverage of choice for at least an hour after you wake up.
- Eliminate or minimize your caffeine intake after the sixth hour you are awake, so your sleep pattern later that night is minimally impacted.

Minimize alcohol: Alcohol is considered a drug that slows down brain activity. It interferes with the brain's communication pathways, affects how your brain processes information, and it is classified as a Central Nervous System depressant. In other words, alcohol literally weakens the mind.

This is not intended to be a lecture on not drinking. Having a drink from time to time is unlikely to cause long-term mental health problems. However, alcohol affects your mood, memory, and ability to think clearly, so consider the aggregate impact alcohol has on your mental health and success.

Have you considered how even your sleeping pattern is negatively impacted? Have you thought about the lost productivity in the days that follow as your recover from your hangover? What about the slower start to your Monday? What about ending your Friday early so you can start drinking?

Long-term excessive alcohol use can result in learning and memory issues, which can lead to the development and exacerbation of mental health conditions, including depression and anxiety.

All of this adds up to a lot of lost productivity time and suppressed mental capacity, just from alcohol.

Mentally strong and successful people recognize this and minimize their alcohol intake. This gives them more time than others to be productive. It provides them the ability to conquer life's challenges with a clear head and keep their mind and memory sharp for the future. Consider the following successful people who've chosen to abstain from alcohol:

- Warren Buffet, one of the most successful investors, said, *"It is one of the reasons why I'm able to perform a cut above the rest."*
- Bradley Cooper, an Oscar-nominated actor and Grammy Award winner, said, *"I don't drink anymore. I realized I wasn't going to live up to my potential, and that scared the hell out of me."*
- Pharrell Williams, a Grammy Award-winning music artist, said, *"Everybody else can do what they want, but that stuff isn't for me."*
- Jennifer Hudson, a singer and actress, said, *"Nobody ever believes me, but I've never had a drink in my life. I'm sober."*
- Donald Trump, the 45th President of the United States, said that instead of ordering an alcoholic drink, *"I just order a Diet Coke."*

- Larry Ellison, a co-founder of Oracle, said his reason for abstaining from alcohol is, *"It clouds my mind, that is reason enough."*

Mentally weak people think being sober will cost them valuable social, networking, and business opportunities. But it won't.

Regardless of the situation you are in or feelings of peer pressure you may be facing, the technique you can use to minimize the amount of alcohol you consume is just being **proud** of your decision and communicating it.

Doesn't this sound familiar to some of the techniques you learned in the chapter, "Find Your Purpose"? You must first define your values. If you want to improve your mental health and live up to your full potential, you'll want to minimize drinking. Then, share your story if you find it helpful. Communicate your decision to others to help keep you motivated and accountable to follow through on your commitment.

At the end of the day, it's your life. You need to make a choice and decide what you really want out of it. If you want to achieve great things, you will have to make sacrifices. There is a negative correlation between the amount of alcohol you consume and living up to your full potential. Be aware of all the "fertilizer" you provide your mind. Your mindset and level of success depend on it.

Sunlight = get sunlight and fresh air, literally

Grass needs sunlight. Sunlight is a key driver of photosynthesis, which is how grass produces its own energy for growth.

Your mind is no different. Many studies show that spending time outdoors can increase energy, decrease depression and anxiety, and improve self-esteem. This is because exposure to sunlight increases the brain's release of the hormone serotonin. Serotonin boosts your mood, helps you feel calm, and increases your ability to focus.

Sunlight is a natural and free performance supplement for your mind. Just make sure you don't overdo it. Too much sun can be harmful to the body.

Your goal should be to get at least 30 minutes of fresh air per day. The earlier in the day you get it, the better, so you can experience the mental benefits for more hours in the day.

Just like exercise, your total exposure to sunlight doesn't have to occur all at once. You can break up the 30-minute goal into smaller blocks of time. Go for a ten-minute walk. Take a phone call or work meeting outside. Take your kids to the park to play. Take the trash out. Get the mail instead of your partner getting it. Do some of that yardwork that you've been putting off. Anything you do outside will make your mind stronger.

Weeds, diseases, and insects

Regardless of the quality of your soil or the amount of seed, water, fertilizer, and sunlight your grass receives, you still have to treat the weeds, diseases, and insects to maintain a healthy foundation that supports future growth.

Your mind is no different. Mentally strong people fight off the mental "weeds, diseases, and insects" to maintain mental strength and support future growth. These might include:

1. Being too hard on yourself (weeds).
2. Falling into a comparison trap (diseases).
3. Caring too much about what other people think (insects).

Being too hard on yourself: Your harshest critic is yourself. Each day we all have undesirable thoughts that sprout into our minds.

"I can't do this." "I'm not happy." "I wish my life was different." "I hate my job." "I wish that person liked me." "I'm not cut out for this."

These thoughts are unpredictable, and unfortunately, they're not necessarily preventable. This is just like weeds in your lawn. Weeds are plants growing in undesirable locations at unpredictable times. Initially, weeds are not harmful to your lawn. But if you don't pull the weeds out, they begin to multiply quickly, overrunning your lawn, and weakening it in the process.

The same goes for your mind. These self-deflating thoughts will multiply quickly if you don't remove them from your mind as soon as they sprout.

Don't be so hard on yourself, don't take everything so personally, and don't live in self-pity. These are all weeds of the mind.

Remember that it's okay to have these types of thoughts. Everyone has them. The point is, you need to remove them from your mind as soon as possible so your mind is not overrun by them.

One way to do this is to use the "Power of Yet" technique you've already learned. Put simply, try rephrasing the sentence, adding the word "yet," and creating a plan of attack. For example, "I can't do this yet. But I'm going to research the things I'm not familiar with, so I can be more efficient and make better-informed decisions."

Comparison trap: It's a side effect of life to want it all. The comparison trap, which is the habit of measuring your life against others, is a toxic behavior. It's a disease that slowly weakens your mind.

When we see others with more money, status, better looks, or better lives, it is natural to feel envy. This issue is exacerbated by the abundance of social media, advertisements, and clickbait that we encounter daily. Research suggests that approximately 75% of people experience envy toward others in any given year. Social media platforms are particularly effective at evoking feelings of jealousy or envy, as they often showcase carefully selected glimpses into the positive aspects of people's lives. However, it's crucial to remember that social media does not always offer an authentic portrayal of reality. What we see online is often a filtered and curated depiction of others' lives and is not accurate or complete.

Mentally strong people recognize there is a difference between "perceived reality" and "reality." Perceived reality is just a snapshot in time. Reality is your entire life. It is unique to yourself and is never the same between two people.

Weak-minded people compare the perceived reality of someone else's life to their own realities. But comparing perceived reality to reality is an apples-to-oranges comparison. Even if you spend every second with somebody, there is always going to be some part of them that is a mystery, regardless of your perception. You will never fully know what goes on in someone else's mind and the real challenges that person is going through in his or her reality.

Mentally strong people stay focused on their own path. They don't allow the perceived reality of others to influence the reality of their own lives. They know it's not an apples-to-apples comparison.

Remember, no matter what you see and no matter how well you know others, it is only your perception of their lives.

Caring too much about what other people think: Many people fail to make their dreams a reality because they care too much about what other people think. The truth is, you will never be able to please everyone. The more you try to please others and live according to their expectations, the more they will control your life, and the more burned out you will become.

> *"You could be the sweetest peach in the world, and there will still be someone who hates peaches."*

Truly successful people are not concerned with what other people think or say about them. Consider Martin Luther King Jr. Do you think he would have been able to achieve the level of success and historical changes he caused if he was focused on pleasing everyone in the process?

People pleasing is like insects in your lawn. The more insects in your lawn, the more energy and nutrients will be consumed from your lawn, which limits your lawn's ability to thrive.

Your life is no different. The more people you try to please, the more energy and focus are taken away from achieving your goals and your ability to make high-quality decisions.

To be clear, this technique is not about disappointing everyone in your life. You still need to maintain high-quality relationships that you value to build mental strength and have success. It's just a reminder that it is okay to not please *everyone.*

To break free from people-pleasing habits, consider applying the principles of the punch card technique discussed in the chapter, "Silence the Noise." This technique requires you to be highly selective and intentional with the people in your life. Choose the 20 individuals who hold opinions that truly matter to you and whose opinions have a significant impact on your behavior and actions. This could include family, friends, coworkers, clients, or anyone else you care about.

Once you have filled all the slots on your punch card, people who don't make the cut shouldn't overly concern you. Their opinions should carry less weight, and you should feel less compelled to please them. By prioritizing the people on your punch card, you can take control of your actions and make decisions based on your own values and priorities, rather than seeking to please everyone around you.

If you do have to disappoint others on your journey to success, do it with kindness but firmness. Life is too short to let others' opinions influence what you do. Only you will completely understand your goals and values.

Mentally strong and successful people decide what they should do and then act on it. They know success does not occur without ruffling a few feathers. They don't agree with everyone just to agree. They don't apologize for things that aren't their fault. And they are able to say no to others.

Cutting the grass = reflection and evolution

Everything we have discussed thus far in this chapter and this book has been related to growth. But when your grass growth goes unchecked, it begins to grow unevenly. Grass that gets too long is problematic because it looks overgrown, is unsightly in appearance, and traps moisture in areas which allow fungus and disease to spread. Therefore, routine grass-cutting is essential to maintaining a healthy lawn.

Your mind is no different. Building mental strength does not mean constant linear growth. The most successful people grow a little but consistently cut some of the growth through reflection and evolution. It's okay to take two steps forward and one step back to reflect.

Arianna Huffington, a co-founder of the Huffington Post, prioritizes reflection as a way to connect with one's wisdom and creativity. Billionaire Ray Dalio credits reflection as the skill that helped him build one of the world's largest hedge funds. He has

said, "*The key to success is knowing how to struggle well. Pain +*
reflection = progress." Confucius, the influential Chinese
philosopher, believed that reflection is the most noble way to
learn wisdom.

Every week, set aside some time to reflect on your experiences
that week. Think about what went well, what you accomplished,
what you learned, what you failed at, what could be improved,
and your feelings throughout the process. For example, many
accomplished business executives, including Rosalind Brewer,
CEO of Walgreens, designate Friday afternoons as a weekly
reflection period to ponder over their accomplishments,
shortcomings, lessons learned, areas for improvement, and
emotions throughout that week.

After you've reflected, think about how you can prepare for
future experiences and plan your goals for the following week.
For example, what would you do differently the next time you
face a similar situation? What did you find helpful that you would
do again? What do you need to stop doing? What do you need to
learn to handle a similar situation better?

Prioritizing a habit of reflection and evolution provides you
with the best opportunity to reach your full potential. Remember,
if you take two steps forward and one step back, you are still
moving forward.

Proper balance = don't overdo it

What do you think would happen if you provide your lawn
with too much soil, seed, water, fertilizer, or sunlight, or cut it too
much? If you worked on it 24 hours a day, seven days a week,
then it wouldn't have any time to grow.

This is the same fatal flaw in weak-minded and unsuccessful people. They think to be successful, they need to be productive 24 hours a day, seven days a week.

It's understandable because, in this fast-moving world, it may feel like you will fall behind if you aren't always working. But if you overdo it, at some point your mind will burn out.

Successful people balance all the essential components of "taking care of their lawn" over the long term. They do not overdo it in the short term. Mental strength and success come from *balanced consistency*, not short-term intensity. Consider this comment from Richard Branson, founder of Virgin Group:

"Success without balance is not success at all."

So how can you ensure you create enough balance to prevent burnout over the long term? First, it's critical to understand that when we talk about balance, many people often envision a perfect 50/50 split. However, mental strength balance is not about trying to give equal time and attention to every aspect of your life. Rather, it's about ensuring that you give adequate focus to the critical areas of your life, even if that means dedicating less than 50% of your time.

Mental rest is a critical component of success. So give yourself time to mentally recharge every week, every quarter, and every year. This is called "mental time off" (MTO).

You've probably heard of "paid time off" (PTO), which is something most employers provide to their employees. Studies show that employees who take PTO experience less stress, are more productive, and are happier overall.

The same can be said about mental time off (MTO). Mentally strong people ensure they have a proper balance of MTO and use it throughout the year. They take weekends off (if they have a typical work schedule), take days off spontaneously throughout the year, and even take a week or two off at a time to just reset and recharge. The result is that, over the long term, they are more productive.

A recent trend occurring in the business world is the concept of Unlimited Paid Time Off (UPTO). Studies have shown that employees take less time off when they have an unlimited number of vacation days. They feel guilty taking days off because the off days are undefined.

This is the same reason people don't take MTO. They never define an MTO balance that they can use, and therefore they feel guilty about taking MTO.

Give yourself one to two MTO days per week. Think of this as your "mental weekend." Give yourself two to three full weeks per year to go on a mental vacation or take the equivalent of a "sick day." To put this in perspective, that still leaves 70-80% of your year that is not MTO.

MTO days give you time to reset and recharge. Think about it. Your phone needs to be recharged every day, or it can't function. When your computer isn't functioning properly, the first thing you do is reset it.

Your mind is no different. Don't overwork it. Take MTO days. You will be more productive, successful, and stronger as a result.

You have now learned all of the essential elements of taking care of your mind's grass. I will leave you with one final thing to remember: Taking care of your grass over the long term is hard. If it were easy, everyone would do it. But if you work hard at it and stay committed to it, you will find the mental strength and life success that you desire.

"Hard work beats talent when talent fails to work hard."

-Tim Notke

TRAIT 8

BUILD POSIMISTIQ HABITS

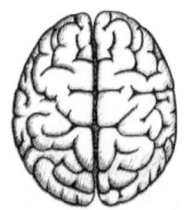

Do you ever wonder why you do what you do every day? Every day from the moment you wake up, you engage in a series of habits that are both good and bad. You might make that cup of coffee or tea the moment you wake up, or immediately check your email, messages, and social media on your phone, even though you did so right before you went to bed.

These habits aren't random. There is a science behind how your habits form or fail to form. In 2012, Charles Duhigg, a graduate of Yale and Harvard, and best known for his book *The Power of Habit: Why We Do What We Do in Life and Business*, explores the science behind habit formation and how individuals can change their behaviors to improve their lives.

In his book, Duhigg discusses what Massachusetts Institute of Technology (MIT) researchers discovered as the "habit loop." The habit loop is a simple neurological loop at the core of every habit, consisting of three parts: a cue, a routine, and a reward.

A cue is a trigger that initiates the habit. A routine is the behavior that follows the cue. And a reward is the positive reinforcement that follows the routine, causing you to crave more of it in the future. These three things create a habit.

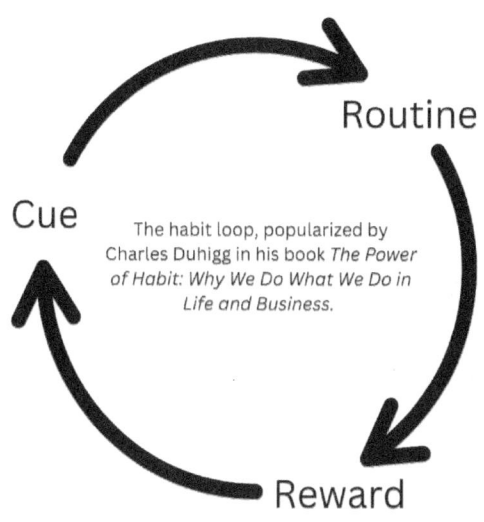

The habit loop, popularized by Charles Duhigg in his book *The Power of Habit: Why We Do What We Do in Life and Business.*

For instance, when you wake up in the morning, the groggy feeling you experience serves as a cue that triggers your routine of making a cup of coffee. The reward is the energized feeling you experience after taking the first sip. The next morning, right on cue, you are likely to go through the same routine of making a cup of coffee to feel energized. This is how your habit is created.

Take a moment to reflect on any habit you currently have, whether it's good or bad. It's likely that your habit consists of the three parts of the habit loop. For example, do you feel the urge to check your phone every time you hear a notification or see an unread message? Do you scroll through social media every night before bed, or snack on junk food when you sit down to watch television?

On the other hand, think about habits you've attempted to adopt but were unable to maintain. It's likely that these failed habits did not include the three parts of the habit loop. For example, trying to read more books, writing in a daily journal, or establishing an exercise routine may have fallen short due to a lack of cues, routines, and rewards.

Duhigg acknowledges that forming or changing some habits can be more difficult than others. But the point is habits evolve from a *process* of cues, routines, and rewards.

So why is this relevant? Up until now, you have learned seven traits and many techniques of the Posimistiq Mind that can help you develop the mental strength needed to live a happier, more successful life. You've just conceived a new mindset that has the *potential* to be strong and successful, but practicing and enforcing that mindset still needs to become a *habit*.

To turn the Posimistiq Mind traits and techniques into a habit, it's not enough to just understand the concept of the habit loop. To increase the likelihood of making it a habit, you need to make the mindset *accessible* to influence your routines, establish a system of *accountability*, and be *consistent* by loving the process more than the potential outcome.

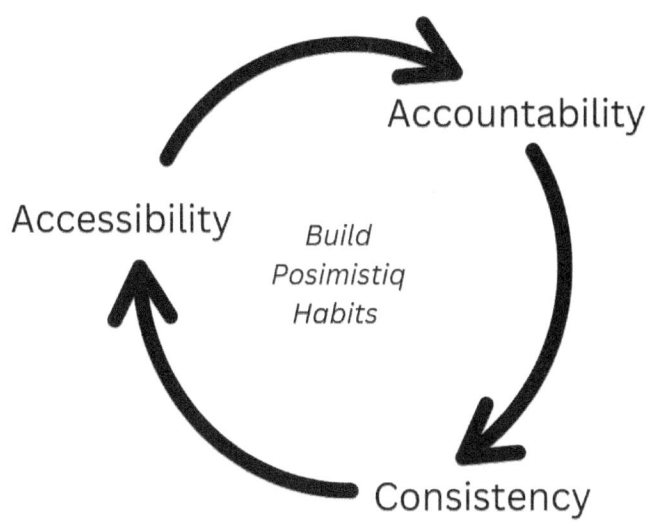

If you don't focus on these core concepts of the process to establish the Posimistiq Mind traits and techniques as a habit, then you've simply read another book without making any lasting changes to your life. Is that what you really want?

Ultimately, creating a habit is a highly individualized process, which is why this chapter focuses on the process itself rather than prescribing a one-size-fits-all solution. It is up to you to determine how to apply the process in a way that is meaningful to you to form, strengthen, and maintain the habit. The more you repeat this process, the stronger the habit will become.

Accessibility

Your routines are your habits in action following your cues. Ideally, the moment your alarm goes off in the morning should be your cue to start your routine of using at least one Posimistiq Mind trait or technique every day to improve your life. As you already learned, the only way to climb a mountain is one step at a time.

However, we all know it's not always that simple. In times of need, your strength is tested the most. This is when drawing on those traits and techniques has the power to influence your life the most.

Therefore, at a more granular level, your specific cues to draw upon your reserves of mental strength are when you are facing your most challenging situations or mental circumstances. When you are feeling stressed, overwhelmed, depressed, tired, emotional, anxious, frustrated, angry, disappointed, hopeless, helpless, insecure, unmotivated, disconnected, scared, or other similar emotions, use these feelings as your cues to trigger your Posimistiq Mindset routine and habit.

During these moments of heightened emotions, it can be difficult to think with clarity and access your inner reserves of mental strength. To make it easier to tap into the mental strength you have developed, recognize that your specific routines are significantly influenced by the concept of accessibility.

Accessibility is a powerful psychological factor that influences action in all aspects of life. For example, stores often strategically place items like candy, magazines, and other small goods near the checkout line to make them more accessible and increase the likelihood of impulse purchases. Having your phone within reach can make it more likely that you'll check social media or engage in other distracting behaviors, even though you're supposed to be working or studying. Having a gym that's easily accessible, such as in your home, can make it more likely that you'll establish a habit of working out, and having healthy snacks within reach can make it easier to maintain a balanced diet.

Habits can be good and bad. Picture your late-night snacking routine. Why does snacking on something at the same time every night bring you comfort, even if you're not hungry or had no intention of eating again after dinner?

Think about it from this perspective. If you have cookies in your home, are you more likely to eat cookies than if you don't have any in your home? When cookies are readily available and in your line of sight, you will feel more tempted to eat them, even if you had no intention of doing so earlier. Your routine to eat cookies is only possible when the cookies are accessible. If they aren't accessible, you wouldn't be eating the cookies!

Your routines shape your habits, not the other way around. So, to build the habit of a strong mind, you must make the traits and techniques a part of your normal routine. To significantly increase the chances of making this mindset a routine, especially when you are feeling stressed, tired, emotional, anxious, or scared, you need to make the mindset *accessible*. Here is how you continuously make the mindset accessible to you:

- Keep this book close by, such as on your desk, nightstand, in the family room, or in your bag.

- Print out the "Posimistiq Mind outline" at the end of this book and keep it in your line of sight.
- Incorporate the portmanteau of Posimistiq in your vocabulary by using it frequently.
- Try teaching another person some or all of the techniques. Teaching keeps the traits and techniques at the front of your mind, which makes them accessible, and it also reveals any gaps in your knowledge that require further review.
- Set a reminder on your phone to be Posimistiq, so you are reminded every time you pick up your phone.

Accessibility is the magnet that attracts routines to desired habits. By doing all these little things, you can make the Posimistiq Mindset more accessible to you, make it a part of your daily routine, and ultimately establish a habit.

Accountability

Rewards provide a positive incentive to repeat good behaviors, while consequences offer a negative incentive to avoid bad behaviors. Without these motivators, you would have little incentive to change your habits. When used together, rewards and consequences create a system of accountability that helps shift your behavior and habits.

Mentally strong and successful people understand the importance of accountability in following through on actions and behaviors to create habits. Consider the words of two personal development experts:

- Bob Proctor, the author of *You Were Born Rich*, said, *"Accountability is the glue that ties commitment to results."*

- Hal Elrod, the author of *The Miracle Morning*, said, *"Accountability is the acknowledgment of responsibility for your actions with the obligation to report, explain, and be responsible for the resulting consequences."*

Without accountability, it's easy to neglect your responsibilities and avoid the necessary actions for progress. This is because it's often easier to make empty promises than to act and hold yourself accountable to a promise.

To put this in perspective, parents often use rewards and consequences when raising children to develop good habits. If children don't finish their dinner, they may not get dessert (consequence), but if they do finish their dinner, they may receive dessert (reward). Without accountability, a child may refuse to develop good eating habits, potentially leading to malnourishment and other health issues.

This is where you are right now. You have made a promise to yourself to incorporate the traits and techniques of the Posimistiq Mind. But it's not enough to simply make that promise to yourself if you want to develop a strong mind and be successful. Without rewards and consequences, the promise is empty.

To truly develop a habit of the Posimistiq Mind, it's essential to establish a system of self-accountability every time you have an opportunity to apply its traits and techniques in your life. While you may have supportive friends and family members, you are your most influential accountability partner. This is because the majority of the work toward building the Posimistiq Mind occurs when no one is watching. The work may go unnoticed by others, making it difficult for them to fully hold you accountable.

Accountability is a personal responsibility that only you can truly fulfill. Therefore, it's important to identify both the rewards and consequences that will drive your behavior toward developing the habit. Rewards should be the things that you find most enjoyable, such as an activity or item. Consequences should be the things you want to avoid or find unpleasant, such as donating to the political party you disagree with.

Remember, when it comes to determining your rewards and consequences, there's no one-size-fits-all approach. What motivates one person may not have the same effect on someone else. For some individuals, the reward for utilizing a Posimistiq Mind trait or technique might be as simple as splurging on a high-end cup of coffee, whereas for others, this may not be enough incentive. Similarly, the consequence for failing to apply these techniques could be the equivalent of putting money into a "swear jar," but whether that's enough to influence one's behavior varies from person to person. The key is to identify the rewards and consequences that truly matter to you. These rewards and consequences will be most effective in developing a habit of the Posimistiq Mind.

Let's put this in perspective by using some of the traits and techniques you've learned from each chapter.

1. *Share Your Story:* Whenever you share what makes you most vulnerable with someone else, buy yourself an

affordable gift (reward). Until that time, do not buy yourself any gifts (consequence).

2. *Find Your Purpose:* When you do something that scares you, celebrate your success with family or friends (reward). If you avoid discomfort by not expanding your boundaries, do a chore during the time you would have spent doing the thing that scared you (consequence).

3. *Silence the Noise:* Every time you find a way to save time over money, reward yourself by spending that time doing something you love like reading a book or watching a movie. If you choose to save money over time, then donate the savings to a good cause so it's like you never saved the money in the first place (consequence).

4. *Develop Resilience and Perseverance:* Place a stack of Post-it Notes on your desk. Every time you see failure as an opportunity and remember that success is a scattered approach, remove one Post-it Note from the pile, symbolizing the mountain getting smaller (reward). Conversely, every time you get frustrated with failure and think success should be linear, add another Post-it Note to the pile, symbolizing the mountain getting bigger (consequence).

5. *Create Your Own Luck:* If you practice something until you can't get it wrong, reward yourself by taking the next day off. If you haven't practiced to this level, the consequence is practicing again the next day.

6. *Learn to be Positive and Optimistic:* Every time you reframe a situation by using the power of the word "yet," transfer some money from your savings account to your

spending account (reward). Conversely, every time you say something to yourself you wouldn't say to someone else, transfer some money from your spending account to your savings account (consequence).

7. *Take Care of Your Grass:* If you follow the 80/20 rule for eating healthy every day over the course of a week, reward yourself with a nice dinner at a restaurant at the end of the week. If you don't follow the rule, the consequence is cooking a healthy dinner at home instead of going out.

Until you identify your most influential rewards and consequences, recall, as discussed in the chapter, "Find Your Purpose," that one of the secrets to staying motivated is to communicate your goals to others. Creating a public commitment to others is a way to subconsciously hold yourself accountable. We all have an internal desire to deliver on our commitments (reward) and a fear of letting down those closest to us (consequence).

Communicate to those closest to you that you plan to incorporate the traits and techniques of the Posimistiq Mind into your daily habits, such as the willingness to take calculated risks, getting at least seven hours of sleep nightly, and making decisions based on the matrix of urgency and importance. By doing this, you will create an external accountability partner who will check up on you from time to time. You just need to take the first step and make that public commitment.

Ultimately, people who succeed at the highest levels aren't lucky. They just have a system of self-accountability to develop good habits. This is illustrated by the following quote from Louis Nizer, widely regarded as one of the greatest trial lawyers of the 20th century:

> *"When a man points a finger at someone else, he should remember that four of his fingers are pointing at himself."*

While some people may say the number of fingers pointing back is actually three, the message remains the same: Before blaming others for our problems, we should also take responsibility and reflect on our own actions and behaviors.

Consistency = love the process more than the potential outcome

There are varying popular notions that it takes a certain amount of time to build a habit, such as a certain number of days. For example, you may have heard that it takes 12 days to make a habit.

In his book, *Outliers: The Story of Success*, Malcolm Gladwell suggests that it takes approximately 10,000 hours of deliberate practice to become an expert in a particular field.

Gladwell based his theory on research conducted by psychologist Anders Ericsson, who studied the training and development of elite performers in various fields, including music, sports, and chess. Ericsson found that those who had become experts had typically put in around 10,000 hours of deliberate practice.

According to Gladwell, the 10,000-hour rule is about a specific type of repetition that involves a focused, intentional effort to improve one's skills. He argues that achieving expertise in any field requires a significant investment of time and effort, and that the 10,000-hour rule can be applied to almost any skill or domain.

However, the belief that there is a magic number that will lead to a habit, such as 12 days or 10,000 hours, is a misnomer.

The reality is the time it takes to develop a good habit is a highly individualized process that depends on the individual and the specific habit. There is no fixed timeline to make a habit, as we are all unique and require varying lengths of time to make a new behavior stick.

For instance, establishing a healthy eating habit may take longer for someone who hasn't previously prioritized healthy eating compared to someone who already consumes a moderate amount of healthy foods. Forming a daily exercise habit may be more challenging for someone who has been sedentary for a long time compared to someone who already engages in some form of physical activity regularly.

Nevertheless, there is one common truth when it comes to forming habits: *repetition is key.* Whether the threshold proposed by Gladwell was 5,000 hours, 15,000 hours, or 20,000 hours, it's the repetitive behavior that emerges from the hours of dedicated practice that ultimately matters. What counts is the repeated effort, which leads to the formation of a habit and its integration into your daily routines.

Successful people do consistently what others do occasionally. Consider comments from the following individuals on the importance of repetition and consistency:

- James Clear, the author of *Atomic Habits*, writes in his book, *"Success is the product of daily habits - not once-in-a-lifetime transformations."*
- Mike Krzyzewski has said, *"Habits are repetitious. Habits must be practiced repeatedly until they become ingrained in your daily routines, and they become you."*
- Wayne Gretzky has said, *"You don't become good because you're good. You become good because you stay committed to the process each and every day."*
- Aristotle once said, *"We are what we repeatedly do. Excellence, then, is not an act, but a habit."*

The same goes for building mental strength and developing the traits and techniques of the Posimistiq Mind. Your journey might be longer or shorter than other readers of this book, so don't set an expectation for yourself that it will take a certain number of hours or days. Consider what James Clear writes in *Atomic Habits*:

"Breakthrough moments are often the result of many previous actions, which build up the

potential required to unleash major change. Imagine that you have an ice cube sitting on the table in front of you. The room is cold and you can see your breath. It is currently twenty-five degrees. Ever so slowly, the room begins to heat up. Twenty-six degrees. Twenty-seven. Twenty-eight. The ice cube is still sitting on the table in front of you. Twenty-nine degrees. Thirty. Thirty-one. Still, nothing has happened. Then, thirty-two degrees. The ice begins to melt. A one-degree shift, seemingly no different from the temperature increases before it, has unlocked a huge change."

Consistency is how you unleash major change and make something a habit. Consistency is the final step that keeps everything connected. Notice how a break in consistency can allow the habit to escape you.

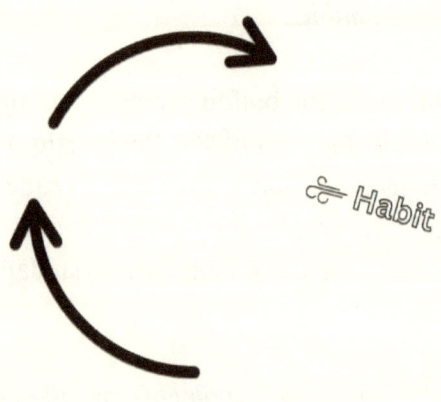

The more you repeat the process, the stronger the habit becomes. But consistency isn't just about repeating the same actions over and over again. Consistency is about loving the process more than the potential outcome to make the process a sustainable part of your life.

Loving the process more than the potential outcome is a powerful tool for building habits and achieving success. Consider this famous quote that has been reiterated by numerous accomplished individuals, including basketball coach John Wooden, motivational speaker Tony Robbins, and mixed martial arts champion Conor McGregor:

> *"Fall in love with the process, and the results will come."*

It is only through a steadfast dedication to the daily habit-building process that you can help yourself reach your full potential!

However, falling in love with the process doesn't happen easily, and it can be challenging to focus on the process rather than just the potential outcome. So how can you truly learn to love the process more than the outcome?

Think of your new mindset like it's your newborn baby, a beautiful new beginning full of potential. A parent's love for a child is often described as the strongest love of all. The love is unconditional, regardless of whether the child is successful or struggling. The parent is fully engaged in the present moment, prioritizing the child's upbringing without getting too caught up in the specific outcome.

The process to raise a child involves a multitude of activities and responsibilities, but it ultimately boils down to one fundamental concept: helping the child form good habits.

Think about this: Children are born with the genetic *potential* to walk but not with the actual *habit* of walking. When children are learning to walk, they don't simply stand up and start walking flawlessly. They stumble and fall. Yet, each stumble is not viewed as a setback, but rather a crucial step in the process of learning and building habits. Most importantly, parents and children remain consistent with the practice until walking becomes a successful habit and second nature.

As simple as this seems, helping children develop good habits is challenging at times. Between countless sleepless nights, endless hours of work, and moments of frustration or discouragement, the most challenging aspect for parents is never really knowing if all the work and self-sacrifice will lead to success and happiness for their children.

Yet, it's the parents' love for their children that ultimately keeps them consistent with the process, every day.

That's where your mind is at today. Just like a newborn, your mind now has the potential to be strong and successful. But without consistent love for the nurturing process, it will never fully develop, make good habits, and reach its full potential.

Start the process now, not later. Remember, later can easily turn into never. If you're struggling to stay consistent, remember that it's easier to form a habit when the behavior is a small, manageable change that can be incorporated into your daily life. Just like a child must crawl before they can walk and walk before they can run, starting with one trait or technique at a time and gradually working your way up to additional techniques over time is a helpful approach. The process is about getting a little bit better each day and staying consistent. It's not about perfection or finishing everything in one day. Consider this comment from Pelé, one of the greatest soccer players of all time, who said:

> *"Success is no accident. It is hard work, perseverance, learning, studying, sacrifice, and most of all, love of what you are doing."*

Love the process of building the Posimistiq Mind habit more than the potential outcome. As you fall into the rhythm of this practice, your mind will begin to crave it, making it easier to stay consistent, and making the Posimistiq Mind a habit.

It's the habit of the Posimistiq Mind that will be the guiding force that helps define your success in ways that are immeasurable, leaves an indelible mark that lasts a lifetime, and unlocks your full potential.

Finally, I will leave you with one quote that masterfully summarizes the connection between process, habits, and success.

"Put simply, success isn't something you stumble upon. Instead, it's a reward for having ceaseless tenacity and <u>steadily</u> working hard. It's a <u>process</u>. It may sound simple but committing to hard work isn't something we learn to do overnight. Hard work is <u>habitual</u>, it takes <u>consistency</u>, and <u>repetitive</u> behaviors to truly submit yourself to the <u>process</u>.

"Many people romanticize <u>success</u>, and even more so, they crave the feeling that they think <u>success</u> will bring them. While it's great to aim high and set your sights on something, this future-focused mentality is actually no use in the present. Instead, it's the <u>habits</u> you have in place right now and your commitment to hitting the mark, that count the most."

-James Cash "J.C." Penny

Good luck on your mental strength and success journey and always remember to be Posimistiq!

ABOUT POSIMISTIQ®

We put mental health at the center of every story.®

Visit our website, www.posimistiq.com, to learn more about Posimistiq, our mission, focus, purpose, and all our products and services.

Stay connected with us by following @Posimistiq on Instagram to stay updated on our future creations and productions.

The power of your reviews and recommendations

I would be deeply honored if you took the time to share this book with others and write a review online. Word-of-mouth recommendations are incredibly powerful and can help us reach people who may not have been aware of our mission.

Your recommendation not only has the power to change someone's life that you directly know but also can impact others you never thought you could help as it spreads through each person's network. Thank you for your invaluable contribution to this cause.

www.posimistiq.com

Instagram: @Posimistiq

Your Feedback Matters

THE POSIMISTIQ MIND OUTLINE

Practice for progress, not perfection.

1. **SHARE YOUR STORY**
   a. Cut through the vulnerability paradox
   b. Never watch a scary movie alone
   c. Sharing your weakness does not make you weak
   d. You could save someone you love
   e. There's no wrong way to share your story
2. **FIND YOUR PURPOSE**
   a. Three-way intersection
      i. What do you enjoy?
      ii. What are you good at?
      iii. What breaks your heart?
   b. Do something that scares you every day
   c. Put on your "gap" glasses
      i. Legacy
      ii. Eulogy
   d. The secret to staying motivated
      i. Write it down
      ii. Communicate it to others
   e. Always live up to your own expectations
3. **SILENCE THE NOISE**
   a. Relentless focus
   b. Master time management
      i. Invest in time blocking
      ii. Buy time
         - Budget money to save time
         - Eliminate distractions

- Delegate
- Declutter by saying "no"

 iii. Decide using the matrix of urgency and importance

4. DEVELOP RESILIENCE AND PERSEVERANCE

 a. Success is not linear; it's scattered

  i. Be happy with failure

 b. Think like a mountain climber

  i. Define your mountain

  ii. Visualize

  iii. Think long term

  iv. The only way to climb a mountain is one step at a time

  v. Expect adversity

- Trough of sorrow
- Self-doubt
- Criticism

 c. Always finish what you start

5. **CREATE YOUR OWN LUCK**
   a. Success is not a percentage game
   b. Take calculated risks
      i. Anticipate opportunities
      ii. Understand odds and probabilities
      iii. Do the high-level aggregate math
      iv. Objectively consider the range of possible outcomes for each individual risk
      v. Overcome analysis paralysis
   c. Prepare
      i. Preparation*timing = luck
      ii. Don't practice until you get it right, practice until you can't get it wrong
   d. Socialize
   e. Remove your emotions
   f. Develop resilience and perseverance
6. **LEARN HOW TO BE POSITIVE AND OPTIMISTIC**
   a. Live in the width
      i. Mindfulness
   b. Don't say anything to yourself that you wouldn't say to others
   c. Reframe your thoughts with the power of the word "yet"
   d. Get on the right bus
   e. Find the silver lining
7. **TAKE CARE OF YOUR GRASS**
   a. Soil = set your foundation
   b. Seeds = plant your commitments
   c. Water = the "learning never ends" mindset

   i. The 8% goal
  d. Fertilize = self-care
   i. Sleep
   ii. Exercise
   iii. Nutrition
  e. Sunlight = get sunlight and fresh air, literally
  f. Weeds, diseases, and insects
   i. Being too hard on yourself
   ii. Falling into the comparison trap
   iii. Caring too much about what other people think
  g. Cutting the grass = reflection and evolution
  h. Proper balance = don't overdo it
   i. Take Mental Time Off (MTO)

8. BUILD POSIMISTIQ HABITS

  a. The habit loop: cue, routine, reward
  b. Accessibility
  c. Accountability
  d. Consistency
   i. Love the process more than the potential outcome

REFERENCES

Centers for Disease Control and Prevention. (2022, April 14). Retrieved from https://www.cdc.gov/alcohol/fact-sheets/alcohol-use.htm

Clear, J. (2018). *Atomic Habits.* Penguin Publishing Group.

Cognitive Behavioral Therapy Los Angeles. (2015, June 5). Retrieved from https://cogbtherapy.com/cbt-blog/common-cognitive-distortions-negative-filtering#:~:text=Negative%20Filtering%20is%20a%20common,allowing%20in%20the%20negative%20information

Covey, S. R. (1989). *The 7 Habits of Highly Effective People.*

Deane, S. (2022, January 4). *Stratos.* Retrieved from https://www.stratosjets.com/blog/fear-of-flying-statistics-trends-facts/

Duhigg, C. (2012). *The Power of Habit: Why We Do What We Do in Life and Business.*

Emamzadeh, A. (2021, May 18). *Psychology Today.* Retrieved from https://www.psychologytoday.com/us/blog/finding-new-home/202105/the-most-common-causes-heartbreak

Eva Selhub, M. (2022, September 18). *Harvard Health Publishing* . Retrieved from <https://www.health.harvard.edu/blog/nutritional-psychiatry-your-brain-on-food-201511168626>

(2016-2023). How I Built This. (G. Raz, Interviewer) National Public Radio.

Information, C. (2022, November 23). *Women's Brain Health.* Retrieved from Staying Hydrated Boosts Brain Power: https://womensbrainhealth.org/think-tank/brain-buzz/staying-hydrated-boosts-brain-power

Lee, J. (2020, December 14). *Sobriety Hacker.* Retrieved from 8 Billionaires Who Don't Drink Alcohol :

https://www.sobrietyhacker.com/fact-sheet/billionaires-who-dont-drink-alcohol/

MasterClass. (2015-2023). Retrieved from www.masterclass.com

Merle, A. (2017, December 6). *Huffpost.* Retrieved from https://www.huffpost.com/entry/exercise-habits-of-ultra-successful-people_b_8900354

Nall, R., & Legg, PhD, T. (2019, April 1). *Healthline.* Retrieved from https://www.healthline.com/health/depression/benefits-sunlight#_noHeaderPrefixedContent

Parisi, T. (2019, October 31). *Addication Center.* Retrieved from Is Alchohol A Drug: https://www.addictioncenter.com/community/is-alcohol-a-drug/

Savin, J., & Biggs, J. (2023, March 10). *Cosmopolitan.* Retrieved from 27 proudly sober celebrities who say quitting alcohol changed their lives: https://www.cosmopolitan.com/uk/body/health/a333232 77/sober-celebrities/

School, W. S. (2019, May 22). *USGS.* Retrieved from The Water in You: Water and the Human Body: https://www.usgs.gov/special-topics/water-science-school/science/water-you-water-and-human-body

The Giving Pledge. (2023). Retrieved from https://givingpledge.org/about

Wikipedia. (2022, December). Retrieved from https://en.wikipedia.org/wiki/Eric_LeGrand

ABOUT THE AUTHOR

Scan the QR code or visit our website at www.posimistiq.com to learn more about Ali G. Moghadam.

About Ali G. Moghadam

"My ultimate goal in writing this book is to have a positive impact on at least one person's life. If my words can bring about change or offer hope to even one individual, it would have been worth every moment spent creating it."

-Ali G. Moghadam